RETRACING THE JOURNEY

RETRACING THE JOURNEY

Teaching and Learning in an American High School

Leila Christenbury

FOREWORD BY
Deborah Appleman

Teachers College
Columbia University
New York and London

Published by Teachers College Press, 1234 Amsterdam Avenue, New York, NY 10027

Library of Congress Cataloging-in-Publication Data

Christenbury, Leila.
    Retracing the journey : teaching and learning in an American high school / Leila Christenbury ; foreword by Deborah Appleman.
        p. cm.
    Includes bibliographical references and index.
    ISBN-13: 978-0-8077-4805-3 (pbk. : alk. paper)
    1. High school teaching—United States.   2. Education, Secondary—United States.   3. High schools—United States.   4. Learning—United States.
5. Teaching—United States.   I. Title.
    LB1737.U6C44 2007
    373.1102—dc22

                                                                2007014354

ISBN 978-0-8077-4805-3 (paper)

Printed on acid-free paper

Manufactured in the United States of America

14   13   12   11   10   09   08   07   8   7   6   5   4   3   2   1

To
John Allen Rossi

colleague, friend, and brother
whose example and wisdom
have enriched both my teaching and my life

CONTENTS

FOREWORD

In *Teacher Man,* a searingly honest account of his thirty years of public school teaching in New York City, Frank McCourt (2005) claims that teaching is "the downstairs maid of professions," the lowest rung on the ladder. He was wrong about one thing: Teacher educators are on an even lower one than the teachers they train.

You've heard the old saw, haven't you? Those who can, do; those who can't, teach; those who can't teach, teach teachers. Recent reports such as *Educating School Teachers* by Arthur Levine (2006) decry the current state of teacher education as being ineffective, anachronistic, and irrelevant to the state of today's schools. In fact, an entire chapter of the Levine report is called "The Pursuit of Irrelevance." Critics of teacher education assert that those who teach teachers are out of touch with the realities of today's classrooms and ill-prepared, both experientially and intellectually, to the challenges of preparing tomorrow's teachers.

These critics haven't met Leila Christenbury.

As you will soon discover, Leila Christenbury offers the strongest possible counterargument to such negative rhetoric about teacher education. In the beautifully written chronicle you are about to read, she demonstrates that, at bottom, good teacher educators have the heart, the soul, the courage, and the persistence of the thousands upon thousands of good teachers that comprise the core of our nation's public schools. Teacher educators *are* teachers. Period. And this teacher educator's journey proves it.

In this book, Leila chronicles her courageous decision to return to high school teaching after a long and distinguished career as a teacher educator, scholar, editor, mentor, and president of the National Council of Teachers of English. I know how hard this is to do. I tried it myself

(Hynds and Appleman, 1997; Appleman, 2003). There is nothing more humbling, and potentially humiliating, than walking one's very public talk, putting one's professed and published methods to the messy and unpredictable classroom test. If, as some have argued, teacher education is no more than a fragile theoretical house of cards, then there appears to be no more certain way to topple it than to put it to the gritty empirical test of real live kids in real classrooms. Yet, as Leila well knows, our theory is useless if it remains untested. And our mettle as teachers rusts without challenge.

Yet it is more than Leila's willingness to return to high school teaching that is laudatory. It is that she matches McCourt in her willingness to recount the ups and downs (with more downs than ups) with unflinching honesty. This is not the narrative arc of the heroic myth in the setting of a classroom—the teacher as savoir motif—that abounds in memoir and film: *Blackboard Jungle, Up the Down Staircase, Dangerous Minds, Stand and Deliver*, and recently *Freedom Writers*. This is not a classroom journey with a heroic and happy ending. But that is precisely what makes it even more important.

In her return to high school teaching, Leila rediscovers the unconquerable complexity of teaching. She is painfully reminded of how many external factors conspire to impinge on the best laid lesson plans —whether it's the counterintuitive structure of the school day, the political landscape of a particular school, or the increasingly ominous shadow cast by state-mandated tests. Leila is brave and perceptive enough to resist the siren call of simple stories with heroic teachers, adoring students, and happy endings. She painstakingly records the nuanced realities of the classroom in Trailer 11:

> There was in this classroom a quiet but consistent opposition of values and of disagreement on what matters, what is worth effort and engagement, and what is not. The way that conflict emerged, how it manifested itself, and how it was ultimately left unresolved is at the heart of this book.

By resisting the oversimplified and perhaps sugar-coated version that would have tempted many of us, Leila makes her journey our own, on that can truly inform and improve our practice by reminding us that between the heroic and disastrous, lies the playing field of most classrooms.

While Leila Christenbury's return to high school teaching in Trailer 11 might have been less than triumphant, this detailed and heartfelt recounting certainly is a triumph of narrative writing and reflection. All of us who believe the heartbeat of democracy is synchronized to the heartbeats of our nation's public school teachers will benefit greatly from Leila's hard-won insights.

Why, it's reason enough to be proud to be a teacher educator.

Deborah Appleman

REFERENCES

Appleman, D. (2003). "Are you makin' me famous or are you makin' me a fool?" Responsibility and respect in representation. In S. Greene & D. Abt-Perkins (Eds.), *Making race visible: Literacy research for cultural understanding* (pp. 71–85). New York: Teachers College Press.

Hynds, S. and Appleman, D. (1997). Walking our talk: Between response and responsibility in the literature classroom *English Education*, 29(4), 272–294.

Levine, A. (2006, September). *Educating school teachers.* The Education School Project. Available on line, retrieved March 26, 2006, from http://edschools .org/teacher_report.htm

McCourt F. (2005). *Teacher man.* New York: Scribner.

PREFACE

This is an account of my teaching English to 22 high school students one recent spring semester in a suburban American high school. It is an account both of what happened and what did not happen. It is anthropological, individual, and based on the premise that the classroom in which I taught and the students there are in some important ways a microcosm of many high school classrooms in many places across America.

In this book I present an interpretation, a generalization that in this one place (which I call Live Oak High School), for this one brief period of time, with one teacher and 22 students, certain things did and did not occur and for certain reasons. There was, actually, none of Charles Dickens's predictable best of times and worst of times. It was far more nuanced: There was in this classroom a quiet but consistent opposition of values and of disagreement on what matters, what is worth effort and engagement, and what is not. The way that conflict emerged, how it manifested itself, and how it was ultimately left unresolved is at the heart of this book.

That conflict regarding what matters most leads, at least from my teacher's perspective, not only to disappointment—for despite my best efforts my students largely preferred not to commit to any sort of sustained intellectual engagement—but to a renewed belief in the urgency for educational change. Until there is more consensus on what matters most in teaching and learning, until there is some sort of shared agreement regarding the *why* of high school education, experiences such as mine in Trailer 11 at Live Oak High School will continue as the norm, not the exception. The promise of education will not be fulfilled. And the losers will be many: teachers who leave the classroom discouraged that their efforts and enthusiasm are irrelevant and young people who are not disturbed or even challenged to move beyond the safe confines provided by enabling schools and a complacent society.

Good enough is not enough. The high school classroom can be a place of challenge and engagement and real learning, and when it becomes simply a barren way station before college, a locale to pass the time, turn the pages, and get the credit, the promise of education is broken.

Our society and our students deserve better. Our high schools can transform. And our teachers can be catalysts for real education that is both challenging and rewarding for all.

ACKNOWLEDGMENTS

This account is the most complex and difficult writing I have ever attempted, a story that was very hard to tell honestly, and it has taken not just time but real effort to think through what happened during my return to high school teaching and why it happened. Starting as a return to fix an aborted article, it became something far more complicated and convoluted as I attempted to make sense of a semester teaching 22 students in a suburban high school. Using some time I had to write during a visiting professorship at the University of North Carolina at Chapel Hill, I went through numerous drafts and revisions of prose, theme, organization, and constant reconsideration of just what returning to high school teaching meant. The article was abandoned and, in many versions and forms, a book emerged.

I have many people to thank. In particular I am appreciative of my very talented and forbearing editor, Carol Collins of Teachers College Press, who has helped me shape and prune this manuscript in areas both small and large. I thank also Kathy Egawa, formerly of the National Council of Teachers of English; Lorraine Rand of the Governor's School in Richmond, Virginia; and the two teachers, Kasey and Terry, of the large suburban high school in the mid-Atlantic, for their generous help with my teaching endeavors and their review of this manuscript. My outside reviewers were specific, targeted, and generous in their suggestions and admonitions; I thank Tom Newkirk, Ruth Shagoury, and Joe Merriam.

Most significantly, my friend and colleague Deborah Appleman of Carleton College has read and discussed this manuscript with insight and wisdom. I thank her for her time, her scholarship, and her sympathetic stance. Perhaps more than anyone she understood the difficulty of what I was trying to convey and helped me get far closer to the mark than I would have been without her. She has been, for this manuscript, my soul sister, and I am in her debt. Her contribution to this book in the Foreword is also most appreciated.

John Rossi, to whom this book is dedicated, has been a colleague and friend during the past 15 years, and his commitment to the classroom and to his students has helped guide my thinking and my writing. For lending books, an ear, and for reading drafts and responding honestly, I thank John. He is a brother, a colleague, and an inspiration to me.

On the home front, Tucker has listened sympathetically to my stories of Live Oak High School and Trailer 11 and to my struggles with this manuscript. To him I give many thanks; he has the patience of a saint, and his accepting nature has provided me an invaluable sounding board.

Finally, I also would like to acknowledge my daily writing companions, who jump up on my desk, peek around the computer monitor, try to walk on the keyboard, leave fur and paw prints on my notes, bark, drop toys at my feet, and generally interrupt me with their version of real life. For their distraction and unintentional moral support, I thank Livvie, Doodlebug, Annie, and Amelia. Like many aspects of the material world, they help keep me grounded.

WHAT MATTERS MOST

The goal is educating, and that means knowing what we're educating for. Purposes must be decided upon. As long as we avoid defining "why," our educational talk rings hollow.
—Deborah Meier, *The Power of Their Ideas* (1995, p. 163)

I taught high school English for five years and then gradually moved into university teaching where I now teach those who wish to be teachers. Although I am sure there are some who have broader experience, I have been an instructor in one sort of classroom or another for almost 30 years. I have taught in a traditional September–June public high school, summer school, parochial school, gifted school, all-girls' school, community college, college, university, and even school in a city jail. Regardless of school level or setting, I have found the work uniformly fascinating, and I have written and researched all my professional life regarding the teaching and learning of English.

These days I work each year with about 20 people who have degrees in English and want to be high school teachers. They teach and observe in local middle and high schools and take my graduate courses and seminars. When those 20 people each year finish the program, they are state-certified secondary English teachers with bachelor's (in English) and master's (in education) degrees. The work with them is wonderful, but it is also somewhat removed from its focus, the high school. And while I have consistently been in the schools with my students and have even done some guest teaching at both the middle and high school levels, it had been many years since I had had my own class of high school students.

This nagged at me. It became increasingly important to return to teach in a high school, to retrace the journey, and I came to the experience that informs this book with some of the highest expectations I have ever had in my professional life. I did almost a year of extensive prior work before I began my spring semester at Live Oak High School with two Live Oak teachers, Terry and Kasey* (both of whom had been my students in previous years), and with them I planned, worked, and collaborated, and got to know the students I would be teaching. Terry was the group's fall semester teacher, and I would take over in spring. Kasey was the chair of the Media Literacy Department and had been immeasurably helpful arranging the teaching, book ordering, and all other details regarding my coming work. This was really important; my university administrators did not object to the teaching, but there was little enthusiasm or support for this venture, and I was very much on my own. Yet my vision of why this was important and my personal link to Terry and Kasey—both of whom were enthusiastic and helpful —fueled me on. I anticipated many things, most of them positive. With prior work and planning, with my own professional background and desire, I was in no way assured of success, but I felt I knew the teaching territory and the possible challenges well.

I was mistaken. I did not assess the setting, the context, or even my students well enough to succeed—at least on certain terms that will be defined later. What mattered to me did not matter to my students, and what mattered to the school and even to the parents was not in synch with my vision of teaching and learning. The promise that I saw regarding teaching and learning was not fulfilled. And the news was mixed: Nothing happened in the classroom that was impossible, dramatic, or irremediable. The classes were never a disaster, but they were something far worse. Ultimately, the classes went—but did not go well. The curriculum was covered, many of the students' grades were respectable, and there were no disciplinary events or crises. But the students were wise in the ways of school and virtually indifferent to my wiles. Although there were exceptions and some brief good times, my students were largely disconnected, uninterested, and waiting for the bell to ring and the next thing to come down the pike. For much of the

---

*The names of the teachers and students are all pseudonyms, and the school and school district are similarly disguised. All student communications are reproduced as written with no effort to regularize spelling, punctuation, or syntax.

semester they showed little real interest in each other, in me, and in what we did or read. They were not about to become intellectually engaged in a sustained manner, and somehow I not only had failed to plan for that, but when I realized it, I was unable to change it significantly. I just held on.

At the end, I was not skillful enough to change significantly the course of events one spring semester or to resolve the conflict of values. But I was determined enough to complete the experience and, afterward, to examine what happened and why.

To what extent can any teacher transform a classroom? During my spring semester I think I did some good, am fairly confident that I did little harm. But the level of engagement, the essence of much of what is important in English class, the essence of what I dreamed and worked for, was never achieved; in fact, it was consistently, routinely resisted. The result was that I—like many teachers, I suspect—had to settle for a far different level of achievement and interest. Despite my efforts to adjust and change during the semester, I was unable to make the teaching and learning experience any measurably different—either for myself or my students—and I came to confront a daily sense of limitation and failure. What mattered to me, what I thought I could "sell" to my students as part of the intellectual life, was not persuasive. What mattered to the school, however, was clear, and was directly related to test scores and compliance. What mattered to most of the parents was equally clear: Understandably, their children's happiness was paramount, but also important was their children's undisturbed sense of being perhaps not the best but certainly very good indeed.

The experience was, most obviously, humbling, and it has provided me with new insight regarding the issues of school, teachers, and teaching. Marilyn Cochran-Smith (2006) says it well: "Teachers cannot fix everything, even if we hold them accountable for everything" (p. 25).

This book is an effort to make sense of a return to high school teaching where preparation, planning, enthusiasm, and skill were often not enough to ensure teaching satisfaction—and, perhaps more to the point, visible and significant student engagement, if not learning. For all my stutters and mistakes as a beginning teacher almost 30 years ago, what fueled me day after day was real student engagement—sometimes instituted by myself, but often manifested without much help from me.

My students in the two high schools where I taught early in my career were hardly scholastic or behavior models; they were often socially inept, poorly dressed, stoned, profane, occasionally violent, and some were clearly emotionally disturbed. But somehow I recall that they were mostly aware and lively students. They challenged me and each other, and there were events in the classroom that were memorable and intellectually as well as emotionally real. I wanted to retrace that journey, but I can honestly write that despite everything I tried, that kind of engagement almost never occurred in Trailer 11 at Live Oak High School.

This experience was disturbing not only for the duration of the semester, but because I was a teacher who got to walk out at the end. Once I turned in my grades at the finish of the semester, I was done with my work and did not have to return. For many of today's high school teachers, there is no such exit such as I had. It seems important to consider what happens when the work of committed instructors, who pour into their teaching what they believe matters most, is not valued or is not successful.

And the culprits are multitudinous. At my most pessimistic, I question: *Do we, in the end, get the schools we deserve?* Certainly we may and, through an implicit contract, weave a web of fictions and evasions that leaves teachers, students, parents, and the community reassured and also undisturbed. This unwritten contract may well be at the heart of the failure of educational reform at the high school level, a topic that has been consistently at the top of the nation's agenda for some 20 years. Yet our reform efforts, regardless of their shape or philosophy or even funding, seem to have left the American comprehensive high school virtually untouched and unchanged; and many classrooms, such as the one in which I taught, remain places of disengagement, evasion, and broken promise.

The urgency for educational change is clear. Whatever we believe high schools could do for students, they are not currently living up to these expectations. A great deal of this has to do with what occurs in individual classrooms, as well as in the enactment of what many educational writers have called treaties (Powell, Farrar, & Cohen, 1985, p. 66 ff.). It also, from a high school perspective, involves a false idealization of the college model. More on that later. But now to school and my journey in Trailer 11.

2

To School

Teachers are almost entirely dependent on their students for evidence of their own success or failures. Teachers need student cooperation in order to do anything in their classrooms, and they often obtain that cooperating through tacit bargaining.

—Mary M. Kennedy, *Inside Teaching* (2005, p. 16)

I started a journal early in the semester of my return to high school teaching. Some of what I wrote reads like a teenage girl before the night of the prom, some of it sounds like Sally Fields burbling at a long-past Academy Awards ("you like me, you really like me"), but it is, embarrassingly enough, reflective of my feelings. The day before I returned to the classroom as a teacher, I wrote:

> The day before my first day in class was one of the more tense days of my life. It seemed all the jitters and all the anxieties came back: Did I have the right pieces of literature? Did I know what to ask during the discussion? Would I have enough time? Too much time? What if, frankly, they didn't like me? Was I really prepared? Could I remember how to get there? What would happen with my parking pass and ID badge? Were my handouts in order? Did I know the regulations? How would I learn the students' names? What if they didn't like me? What if they didn't like me?
>
> In the early afternoon before the first day, I went to my local Starbucks to pick up some coffee. "Dr. Christenbury, Dr. Christenbury," I heard. And it was Jackie, a student in my class, who had finished exams early and was at Starbucks relaxing with a friend. "You're coming tomorrow, aren't you?" she asked—"we're so excited." Ah, an omen—her open

and friendly face, her direct manner. A good omen. Maybe they'll like me.

I could not sleep the night before I began my teaching. I was close to terrified: What if all this did not work? I tossed, turned, checked the clock and the alarm again and again. Again, from my journal:

> Not much sleep that night, irritable and worried. Got up, did the pets/coffee/get dressed routine, drove, prayed. Would they like me?
> And then they start to come to our classroom, Trailer 11. I am at the door, smiling, talking, joking. I like them, I like them. My voice is choked with morning phlegm at the beginning, but we start the routine. Too many questions. Too much repeated info. Call for order, silence, listen. We hand out, arrange, organize. It's journal entry time, and I write with them. For more than 10 minutes—announced limit—they write and write and write.

The journey had begun.

TRAILER 11

Even with all the whirl of excitement on my first day returning to the high school, I was struck by the physical setting of the classroom where I would be teaching. I would be spending my semester in Trailer 11, an aging portable permanently moored on Live Oak's campus. Trailer 11 was meant, like its 15 sisters, to be temporary classroom space for an overcrowded (2,300 students) high school. Now, after some 10 years, located in a sort of trailer-park camp approximately 100 yards outside the main school building, it was looking rather permanent and, because of steady use, also rather shabby.

I had been a visitor in Trailer 11 for some time before beginning teaching, but now I truly *saw* it. Frankly put, Trailer 11 was in disrepair; its ceiling tiles were discolored, its three small windows crooked in their frames, its linoleum floor uneven and, as I found out during the semester, rarely swept or even washed. Despite a loudly enthusiastic heating and cooling system, Trailer 11 also turned out to be both cold in the winter and hot in the late spring and early summer. Acoustics were not good within, as the space was long and narrow, and the many sharp surfaces seemed to make voices reverberate in an unnatural manner.

The furniture in Trailer 11 was minimal. There was one small corner closet, but it was so narrow that it could not accommodate the width of a standard clothes hanger, so a hook was used for the teacher's coat, and spare textbooks were stacked on the floor. There was a teacher's desk and chair, three bookcases on two different walls, and 22 student desks, all in rows. There was a television on a stand with a tape player, two white boards, a bulletin board, and a speaker on the wall for announcements from the office. There was one laptop computer for the teacher's use but because of the distance of the trailer from the main building, no connection to the Internet, and no connections for student laptops.

The materials handed out by the school to secure the trailer for a disaster—imagine a terrorist with a gun hunting through the school for students—were laughably inadequate. On the other hand, when an errant soccer ball broke one of the trailer windows, leaving glass scattered everywhere, a workman appeared and replaced it within the hour, scrupulously removing all the glass shards and pieces.

Regardless of the drawbacks of the physical space, I was happy to be back in the high school classroom. Trailer 11 was sufficient.

LIVE OAK HIGH SCHOOL

Trailer 11 was located on the grounds of Live Oak High School, a comprehensive high school with a full athletic program, a wide offering of subjects, and an attempt to meet the needs of all its students in both depth and breadth. Live Oak was one of 59 total schools and one of 10 high schools in Martin County School District, a district that served 56,000 students in a mid-Atlantic metropolitan area of one million residents. Using a block schedule, Live Oak offered the standard array of subjects to its students: math, social studies, English, science, career and technical courses, visual arts, performing arts, and dual enrollment for college credit with a local community college. There were basketball and football teams and ROTC. A school of 2,300 students and a faculty of 175, Live Oak's central building was approximately 10 years old, and the student body was largely middle class and approximately 80% Caucasian, 15% African American, and 5% Hispanic, American Indian, Alaskan Native, or Asian/Pacific Islander. English was the first language of most of the students.

WHO THEY WERE

The 22 junior students in my block English class were the very first cohort group in an experimental program within the high school. They had been together for three years as part of the innovative and by-application-only Media Literacy program that was in its own department and had my former student Kasey as its chair. By plan, the students had a number of their classes together—history, English, media literacy—and were designated honors students and also considered "special" by their teachers. They received honors credit for the course and, I was told by their current teacher, Terry, and by the department chair Kasey, were creative if not completely academically inclined. The cohort nature of the group was, however, an unexpected problem: As two students told me privately and quietly during my observing time before I took over the class, they were all moderately sick of each other. Familiarity was breeding contempt: The 22 spent every school day together in multiple classes, and there were serious tensions within the group and defined, hostile cliques, a fact that Kasey and Terry had told me about months before (Terry noted "they know each other so well that it seems like they have taken every class since kindergarten together"). Why this factor did not strike me as more important than it did is, in hindsight, a crucial misjudgment on my part.

The composition of the class was gender-biased, with 19 females and three males; all were designated as college-bound. One student had an Individualized Education Program (IEP). The economic range was working class (a numerical minority in the class) to upper middle class (also a numerical minority). Ethnic background was somewhat varied. Of the 22 students, there were six African Americans, 15 Caucasian students, and one identifiable second-generation Indian. One student was diabetic and needed to leave each class early for blood checks; one was pregnant and delivered her baby at the beginning of the spring semester.

I did some early academic assessment. Of the beginning writing samples that I collected before I began teaching, about six of the 22 students were very skilled writers; my IEP student was bright but severely dysgraphic; and one student appeared to be writing on a fourth- or fifth-grade level. The rest appeared to be writing approximately on grade level. Previous semester grades were not something I wanted to study closely—I did not want to be unduly swayed by that kind of prior information—but at least four students of the 22 were not performing well; Ds and Fs were the norm for them, and they did not, according to Terry, regularly turn in assignments.

Observing the class with Terry as their teacher, I didn't see much that I didn't think I could handle. Yes, the students talked constantly among themselves while Terry was talking (and she talked more than I did in my own classroom), but I knew ways to work with that. And, yes, Terry had come to me early in the previous semester to consult about her own difficulties dealing with the 22; but she was a novice teacher, and I had some ideas, born of experience and knowledge, that I thought would address those difficulties. Yes, as students had just told me, members of the group were tired—even sick—of each other, but my activities and enthusiasm could, I trusted, surmount that fact. The whole issue of establishing a different climate, a different vision of how the class could function was clearly in my sights. At the time, I did not think that starting that new climate in January rather than in September and establishing that different vision might be more difficult than I had imagined. It would be.

WHAT THEY EXPECTED

The first day, I mastered my jitters and tried to set a tone. Although they were familiar with me from my observing and working with them, I wanted to be direct with my new 22 students: honest, authentic. It seemed important to me that they understand that I needed them and that I was prepared to learn from them. I had talked about this before with the group, but during this first class I talked again about why I was here with them this spring. I reiterated what I expected of the students, but said that I also wanted them to know they could also articulate what they expected of me. I even handed out a copy of the piece I had written about what I had learned from teaching (Epilogue from *Both Art and Craft,* Christenbury, 2000, pp. 219–220), and I asked the students to read it in class. They politely complied. Then I handed out a draft outline of the semester and asked for feedback. Students did have some comments, and I took notes.

But I know well that students will often not say what they truly feel if they must speak publicly and in front of the group. So, later in the same class, I asked for anonymous comments on their expectations, feelings, and needs for this upcoming class. I distributed blank index cards and gave students about ten minutes to write. I collected those, took them home, and used them and my notes as I finished the initial planning for the course and finalized the first nine weeks' syllabus.

What mattered to the students? The following is what I received from 20 of the 22 (two did not turn in their cards) when I asked them to write, anonymously, about what they expected from the class:

> Everything's fine with me. I'm really looking forward for this semester.

> I am looking forward to this class because my previous English classes have not been the best learning experiences. I would like to really get into great literature and discuss it all, not just the theme. I would like to thank you for taking the time to teach us.

> Present the literature in an exciting, interesting way. Not expect us to be at the college level of writing/thinking . . . although expect our best! Encouragement.

> I expect to learn in a manner that excites me—and I mean *really* learn! I'd like some help with writing skills and just overall preparation for higher-level learning.

I'm not sure what I expect or want. I do expect a fun semester and to read some great American literature. The field trip and research project sound fun.

All I really expect is that you give us direction, but don't limit us creatively or in our interpretation of the novels. I just hope that you'll embrace the fact that we are all very different people with every different views and interests. Oh, and it'd be nice to read more Jewish-American lit.

Be real. Be understanding. Be fun. Be a strict teacher but ladeback.

I expect a serious class. Some fun. I expect some in depth detail of what we're reading in a discussion. I expect some essays along with the reading, and not too much reading at night. I expect for you to be open-minded to this class. I expect for you to make my second semester a good learning experience.

I expect for you to be a vary good teacher that will help us all learn a lot of things we never knew.

Be flexible. Lots of discussion. Relaxed but still teach. For project we should get to remake part of a novel in our own style and film it.

Teach us how to analyze/interpret literature PROPERLY. Allow us to read quality, sensible books—not just a bunch of new age garbage and a bunch of confusion. Have fun with us and be yourself while we have class discussions/debates. Be open-minded not judgmental and hear and understand our opinions. P.S. Thanx 4 joining us—I look forward to experiencing your lectures/lesson plans!!!!

I'm just excited that I'll finally have a real English teacher. I expect that you can teach me how to actually rite a good paper b/c having [name of previous year's teacher] for two years in English actually sets you back and my teachers in middle school (I went to a ghetto one) always told me that I could improve in high school but I haven't.

I expect you to do what you normally do. Whatever you do, you're the teacher so when you lead I follow.

What you have described sounds wonderful . . . I look forward to your class. P.S. And controversy? Awesome, it's exciting!

Class discussion because it's a good way to get ideas. Peer editing in class for papers we have.

I know your a college professor, so I would like it if you would help us prepare for college English classes and what they expect. Don't be a "stick in the mud" because then the class gets boring and I won't like it anymore. English is one of my favorite classes.

I want class to sometimes be spontaneous. I don't think that everything always needs to be carefully planned and thought out. It would be nice to come in to class and just go totally off from the agenda. Also, I really want to read some of those books you talked about!! P.S. Teach us how to write a real essay!

I expect to be educated on literature. From what I have seen and heard from you, it sounds like we will be exposed to lots of new things. You seem like a great teacher, who really knows and feels the literature. I can't wait to get started. This class also seems very creative and I like that sort of thing.

I think this class will be really fun. I'll read almost anything so literature's not an issue. I enjoy writing but I don't do very well with essays, so if the rate of essays was at a minimum that would be nice. It'd be nice if while we're reading things, we could discuss it, like hidden meanings and things like that. Debates are always fun with this class to. I don't really expect a lot just to have a fun class that's interesting.

In this class I expect a change. I have been lucky to have [previous year's teacher] for the past 2 years, but now I'm ready for new challenges, I don't feel like I learn if I'm not challenged that's why I've always set my goals a little higher and make it harder for me to reach them. I want you to challenge me. In writing I want to be challenged in working on better formats. I feel I have good writing skills and concepts, I just tend to pour it all out sometimes. In reading I want to go in depth in books I feel in high school we skim through novels some times that way I can't enjoy it. Well I look forward to this semester, and any challenges you bring my way.

Some of this was a bit surprising; most was encouraging. I had planned to use video as one student suggested, and the literature titles—which I had previously, briefly described—seemed interesting to the students. I was, however, puzzled to see many students equate my coming to teach them with "college level" work—something I had never mentioned and never intended as a benchmark. Nevertheless, for some students this appeared to be what they expected. I was also surprised to see students describe their previous English classes as not useful or rigorous. This was a negative comment about the work of both Terry and Kasey, who had taught this group in previous semesters, and I decided not to share that negative assessment with either one. I doubt they would have been surprised, but I worried that the students sharing this with me, the very new teacher, would unnecessarily hurt their feelings. In my experience, this kind of retroactive negative assessment is not uncommon; the anticipation of a new start can cause students to discount the influence and work of previous teachers.

THE PLAN

On the other hand, little of what I read in the 20 cards made me wholly reconceptualize or change what was soon to be a syllabus and plan for the first nine weeks of the spring semester. During the fall, I observed in Terry's class and also talked to the students as a whole and, later, with individual students. I studied the school district and school policy manuals and learned how to use the school district electronic blackboard to which Live Oak subscribed and to which all students and parents had regular access. Before the semester started, I wrote and submitted a grant to subsidize a class trip to New York City where, as part of our American literature study, we would visit pertinent sites such as Ellis Island and Harlem.

I had worked on the syllabus for almost a year prior to coming to the class; the study of American literature (including selections from a list of classics), vocabulary, the completion of a research paper, and the taking of two state-mandated tests were all required by the Martin County School District. However, Terry, Kasey, and I had agreed that the spring semester would continue a thematic organization and that, within that theme, I would not only dispatch with the school district–required curricular elements but also add a number of creative projects that would dovetail with the media literacy facet of the students' program.

Because Terry's love of African-American literature had been the focus of the first semester (the students had read Langston Hughes's poetry, *Raisin in the Sun*, *Their Eyes Were Watching God*, among other pieces), I thought the idea of looking at literature written by others in America, those who came to this country in the 19th and 20th centuries and were not brought in slavery, would be a good shift. "Coming to America" became the general thematic title, and under that umbrella we would read literature representing a number of groups. Those included Latinos, Japanese Americans, a number of immigrant groups in 19th-century New York City, and European Caucasians living in the Midwest, the West, the cities, and rural America. I was not interested in using a textbook and decided to gather materials outside the school-district-adopted anthology. We would read novels, short stories, poetry, and nonfiction (essays and reports). I would create handouts with additional literature I thought would be helpful.

Beyond the handouts, the literature would come from the 19th, 20th, and 21st centuries, we would range among classics and contemporary works, and we would include young adult novels. Students would have choices among short stories and novels, and for response there would be essays, group reports, video projects (transforming the short stories into one-minute movie trailers), and a menu of creative projects for the young adult novels (ABC books, creative letters, poetry response).

The ideas kept coming: We would collaborate with a class in another school and school district and study together a classic novel, culminating in a shared Socratic Seminar at the other school. I thought the vocabulary book was useless, and Terry agreed, so I tossed it for the semester and decided that all vocabulary would come from the literature we read. In addition, I would rely on student selection for that vocabulary as well as most test items in the nine weeks' tests. Essays would be workshopped significantly with revision groups and conferences, and we would write in our journals every morning at the beginning of class. The research paper would have a kaleidoscope of choices, all of which related in some way to "Coming to America," including immigrant or historical stories from the students' families, American icons such as the hamburger or the movie star, an American writer we had not studied previously, the day of your birth, and so forth. Presentation of the research papers would be done in a talk-show format with myself as host and the student researchers as guests.

Before the class began, I had outlined this plan to the students, asked for responses from them, and discussed it all with Kasey and Terry. Everyone was initially enthusiastic, and I felt that although it would be a lot of work for all of us, it was a rich array of reading and activities and, more to the point, a concerted effort to make sure students could control their assignments, some of their choice of readings, and the test items to which they could respond.

At the time, working on the curriculum was really exciting. Perhaps Thomas Wolfe was right when he wrote that you can't go home again, but for me this was a long-overdue family reunion.

THE ADJUSTMENTS

After reading the students' cards, I did add a short story by Malamud to respond to the Jewish-American literature request, and I realized that some African-American poetry, even though it had been used in the previous nine weeks, was essential to revisit. It was clear that the immigrant slant was not as compelling as I thought it would be, so I quickly added the idea of "images" of America to the "coming to" America theme to be more inclusive. I put together a packet of prose excerpts, song lyrics, and poetry that I thought would stimulate discussion and divergent viewpoints. The packet included prose excerpts from James Baldwin's chapter "The Discovery of What It Means to Be an American" from *Nobody Knows My Name: More Notes of a Native Son*; the Declaration of Independence, Pledge of Allegiance, and Preamble to the Constitution of the United States of America; an excerpt from Theodore Roosevelt; and selected immigrant recollections. I also added stanzas from Irving Berlin's "God Bless America" and Katherine Lee Bates's "America the Beautiful," as well as poetry from Emma Lazarus's "The New Colossus"; Langston Hughes's "I, Too, Sing America"; Lawrence Ferlinghetti's "I Am Waiting"; Naomi Shihab Nye's "Blood"; and Lawson Fusao Inada's "Kicking the Habit."

In general, I felt I had been apprised of some attitudes, but I also felt that what the students wrote on the index cards was about what I had anticipated.

Looking back at the cards some time later, now that I have taught the class, I think that like most young people, my new students knew well the rhetoric of "challenge." Their responses indicated that they did want that experience, that they wanted to *feel* that they were working hard. It was less clear how hard many of them actually wanted to work. In *The Shopping Mall High School*, Powell, Farrar, and Cohen (1985) cite the concern that

> many students . . . do not learn. They avoid learning. The accommodations made to hold students and keep the peace permit this option. It is easy to avoid learning and still graduate. It is even easy to do so and graduate believing that one has learned. (p. 310)

On the other hand, the students were specifically hopeful that I, the teacher, would provide some interest and excitement. Further—symptomatic of many students—they wanted to learn the "hidden secrets" of literature and the "tricks" of writing a great essay. Oh, and while I was at it, I needed to teach hard but also to be open-minded, laid back, and fun.

I had my marching orders; I made the changes in the syllabus and was determined to try.

3

THE FIRST WEEKS

Teachers play to tougher houses than actors do. They also play to them in more intimate settings, and the schedule run is generally longer, regardless of the reviews. . . . Teachers move among their audiences, address them, converse with them. Any inattention, boredom, hostility is clearly visible before them. Because there are normally no co-stars or supporting players, the experience of teaching imperfectly is essentially a private matter. And again, because failure is by nature humiliating, we tend to keep it to ourselves.

—Richard A. Hawley, "Teaching as Failing" (1979, p. 597)

My first intimation that some of my assumptions were off-kilter was when I did a "get to know" activity that very first week. Because these students had been together as a cohort group for some years, the usual introduce-yourself-to-me-and-to-the-class was pretty lame. *I* was the only unknown here; most of these young people had told me that they knew each other only too well. Just recently, I had picked up a variation of "get to know" that I liked. It was a brief fill-in-the-blank set of statements that began "I'm the only one who _____." It seemed to me that even after all this time together it was possible that the students did not know *everything* about each other, and "I'm the only one who" might open up some new territory, both for them and for me, their new teacher.

MORE THAN I WANTED TO KNOW

So I did a warm-up intro, handed each student a sheet with four or five "I am the only one who _____" statements and gave them about five minutes to think and write something down. I did a sheet, too.

Sharing with a single partner or even in a small group seemed too confining for this class, which knew each other so well, so I invited volunteers to share their comments with the entire group. I would be their auto-scribe and put the array of answers on the board. The responses would, I thought, be a useful snapshot of the variety in the class. I speculated that the sharing might be tentative, that some students might not have much to say, but that it would be useful. The whole thing would probably take ten minutes maximum.

Wrong. The students were delighted to share, to go beyond sharing. If I had been really aware, I would have seen that the way this activity unfolded suggested in some ways that the students had an entrenched and ongoing hostility toward each other, and were determined to show that they and they alone were unusual. Students who shared—and there was a forest of hands—had lists and lists of the ways in which they were the *only one who* (Jackie mentioned about a dozen ways she was utterly distinctive, followed by other students whose lists were almost as long). The board filled to bursting with these confident, at times even outlandish, claims to uniqueness and individuality. Whew —self-esteem did not seem to be an issue here at all. Twenty minutes later, I had to shut down the activity, and the goal of "get to know" seemed almost lost in the bravado of my being the absolutely only one who _____.

Another characteristic of the group that became immediately apparent that first week was their pattern of not listening to me and not listening to each other. As I had seen in observations when Terry taught the class, the students were used to talking all the time, regardless. When we wrote at the beginning of every class in our journals, there was silence. But in the usual turn-taking of small-group reporting and large-group discussions, not to mention during announcements or comments or even brief spurts of informational tidbits from me, there was a consistent, constant undertone of talk. This was something I registered as an issue right away, and I worked on it almost all semester. I rearranged seating and tried all sorts of other strategies to combat the problem: wait time, flicking the lights, direct comments, and positive reinforcement when students seemed to approximate some sort of conversational order. But even at the end of our semester together, despite reminders, halts in the conversation when the sub-talk got too loud, and praise for the few times when students actually listened to me and to each other, the students as a group could not listen for more than one to two minutes to *any* single speaker—peer or myself—without being called back to silence repeatedly. It did not matter to the students in this group, where no one really listened; no one held the floor without side conversations erupting. But it did not fit my pattern of listening and turn-taking; I never talked for long periods, but even then students would not desist from simultaneous conversations. For me, that was a continuing difficulty and a true puzzle, and I could not break the pattern.

WHAT SEEMED IMMEDIATELY RIGHT

Beyond the early jitters and the unexpected, I was thrilled to be back in the high school classroom. I wrote in my journal:

> We move to Images of America. We list. I have someone choose one of the topics from the list. I start a web and the chooser does the first adjective. We continue. I remember many of the names. I smile, I joke, they laugh; the number of hands raised is a forest. . . . We do the activity. There is time.
>
> I give the homework. They are relaxed. I am satisfied. I still have the old mojo. I still have it.
>
> The students leave. Terry, who has been at her desk the whole time, loves it; Kasey comes in and asks how it went. It went well. She grins, we all grin. I am not exhilarated; I am happy it is over, I know it will do well. I am a fit.

One of my first days, I left Trailer 11 and went into the larger Live Oak building and felt, for a strong pulse, the energy and range of a large high school. I liked being in the hall at the change of classes, seeing the students, and even getting a very firsthand look at the severely handicapped students who were located in a center at the high school and whose teachers seemed interesting, on target, and clearly fond of their students. I wrote at the time:

We go to the library and just walking the halls with the two of
them, looking and seeing some of my students sitting in the
cafeteria, I am so excited. Stupid, stupid, but it feels like home. I
eye the other staff members; they nod to me with my ID badge.
I am one of them. I am irrationally excited to be there and to be
part of this large and expansive high school. Kasey can tell what
I am feeling—"You're a high school teacher, Dr. C.," she says.
There is nothing more I want to hear from her. Jesus, I am. I am.
She talks now of my doing this again. And again. I have thought
the same thing.

The first few weeks, working closely with Live Oak's library was
a revelation; there was so much available, and the librarians were eager
and prepared to work with teachers and students. Certainly I loved
the array of resources—so much that I decided to ignore the first day's
stumble when the librarian with whom I was talking startled me. From
my journal:

> To the library. The librarian has things set up so well; it is
> another century indeed. There will be Internet pathways set up
> for the research paper; they are used to this and proud of it.
> Justly so. The librarian knows me from other times and says I
> am the best thing that has ever happened to my university.
> Teases me about my love of YA lit. Flattering, but then she asks,
> "Why are you here? Are you dabbling?" Stops me cold. No,
> indeed, I take this seriously, fully, and tell her so. The chasm,
> which I know well, is there. No, I am not a tourist, not a dab-
> bler. I am the real thing. I am happy to be here. I know that I
> must earn my way. I think I can do it.

The moment passed. I had other work to do, and for the research paper
—which sported five different topic areas and choices within those
areas—the librarians set up search paths and established electronic sites
for citations. The library itself was huge, colorful, and well-stocked, far
more extensive than what I had experienced in my previous years of
teaching. And the supplies seemed generous: The filmed version of
Death of a Salesman with Dustin Hoffman (1985) was right there on the

library shelves, and I could keep it for a month. A technical question I had regarding the school's cybernetwork was answered immediately. This was heaven.

Heaven also included communication. Despite the lack of Internet access in our trailer, students were in the habit of using e-mail, and I had encouraged them to keep in close touch. Beginning the first few weeks and extending through much of the semester, I received inquiries, requests, and, from one student, Helen, what became a pattern of complaints about what Helen thought might be inequitable treatment of her as compared to others. Helen also regularly reported on the less-than-stellar behavior of other students, information she thought I would like. Helen aside, it was helpful to get these e-mails and helpful to be able to respond within a few hours, especially since I was not at the school every day during the week. This kind of communication seemed like a great positive to me.

Overall, my first days returning to the high school classroom seemed promising, especially compared to my earlier teaching experience. My students were better groomed, better dressed, better behaved, and—at least in class when I could see them—drug-free. When I began teaching in the 1970s, the classroom atmosphere could be wild and wooly, often fueled by students who were high on pills and/or marijuana, but in this classroom there was no casual cursing, no fighting, and no overt hostility (at least until later in the semester). By my standards, most dissension was mild. Only near the end of the semester did it become more serious: Helen's displeasure with her peers intensified, she stepped up her reporting of others' behavior, and was openly hostile to other students. Erin and Sharon, who traveled and operated as a team, became more openly scornful of their less-attractive and less-popular classmates. In addition, the class's new mother, Sharonda, was not popular with a small clique of other girls in Trailer 11. The tensions simmered and then escalated, and at the end of the semester, three girls ganged up on Sharonda outside of class, cornering her and shouting, "You're just a slut with a baby." Some of this was racial, no doubt. Sharonda, I was told, just shrugged it off; but those conflicts then moved into end-of-the semester confrontations in Kasey's class with the students.

At the beginning, though, none of this conflict had surfaced. I wonder now if I was holding on to some sort of a utopian illusion, but my journal entries almost ecstatically note that in class, students would tentatively use an unusual vocabulary word, link something they read to something that meant something to them, or read a witty journal entry aloud. I was thrilled. At home, reading their early work during the first weeks in the semester, I noticed passages that were sprinkled with what I felt were inventive turns of phrase, images, and ideas. This was fantastic, the real thing. I found it easy to praise students, and I was exhilarated. During the first month, almost every time I got in my car to head back to the university, I was still talking to them, working with them, thinking about them. Early on, the students in my class were, as I remembered my high school students being years ago, consuming.

STORM CLOUDS

What followed quickly, however, was very different. The first major assignment, an essay based on our discussions and our first readings of the handout with poetry, prose excerpts, and song lyrics was due, and students seemed to panic. They asked for extra class time for a second round of revision groups. No problem; I was delighted that they were taking the first paper so seriously and I was happy to accommodate the request. But during that 90 minutes of the second round of peer groups, it was clear to me that those same students were using the extended class time for purposes other than working on their papers. After the first 10 minutes, they didn't seem to want to work in their revision groups, and when I duly circulated, no one had questions or comments, and it was obvious that they were waiting for me to move on to the next group so they could resume their talking. Oh well. I decided not to make a big issue of it—this was the first paper and the first round of peer revision work.

But worse was to come. When the paper was actually due to be turned in, over a third of the students just didn't come to class that day. Others reported that computer/printer/disk/personal problems prevented their turning in the assignment on time. Just how out of touch was I? Evidently, I was missing a whole lot, as this reaction to the first deadline was, for me, unexpected. More problems ensued beyond difficulties meeting a deadline, and at times, I couldn't believe what was happening. How is it that I didn't see this coming? How is it that I had few innovative coping strategies when it did?

THE DISCUSSION THAT DIED

Deadlines were one thing, but then the class itself seemed to take a turn. It was still early in the semester. This January, we were embarking on a series of days with snow and ice and freezing rain that wreaked havoc with school schedules. The day after school was closed due to snow, my students came to class for a shortened schedule. The predicted ice had not closed school for a second consecutive day, but had just delayed the opening. As a result, we were in class, but instead of having 90 minutes we had 40. As my students entered Trailer 11, I could tell that they were not, from the onset, particularly cheerful. Most had expected to be home for the day, but here we were. Yes, students wrote in their journals with their usual cooperativeness, but they seemed really reluctant to share afterward. Yet I thought it was important that day for someone to read some of their writing aloud. As we had established our pattern, I invited someone to share, and waited. And waited. Finally, LaBelle broke the silence and read, followed by Alice and Helen and others. But it was not good karma; I got the participation I wanted, but the atmosphere afterward was tense.

I didn't want this to just go on without comment or intervention. I asked the students what was wrong. And then there was a small explosion; students were more than happy to talk about what was wrong. They didn't like the literature assignment, it was dumb. They were so fervent about it—and so reluctant to provide "dumb" details—that I realized many had obviously not read what was assigned for that day, in anticipation of school being closed. Sure enough, the large-group discussion was halting and riddled with opinions that appeared to have been taken out of the air, most from the title on the first page of the piece, and not from the interior pages. There was much self-expression but little that related to the text. I persisted, over the obvious evidence of inattention: shifting bodies, combs taken out for grooming, mirrors bought out for makeup touches, furtive private conversations, and passed notes. I called on individual students to read aloud pertinent passages to illustrate their opinions, and I referred to a handout I had made and given to students highlighting quotations from the text. I tried to get students to focus in our shortened class time, but what ensued was a wandering, halting, silence-punctuated discussion. Mercifully, the bell rang.

It was not a good day. And there was little to do but just get through it. Looking back at this class, it is clear that the unexpected first snow day, the students' dislike—or non-completion—of the reading, and the odd schedule all conspired. My persistence and wait time regarding journal sharing backfired, and after that, all my teaching techniques could not quickly create the open, inquisitive atmosphere we needed. Here, as in other times to come, the mojo, even my veteran mojo, just did not work.

And this signaled a shift for me. Somehow in the middle of all my planning and teaching and grading, I had had time to write about my return to the high school classroom and had submitted a wildly happy article to a professional journal about my experience. It had been accepted, and I was doing some requested editing. I knew it was premature to write about my return to the classroom, even in a brief article, but I had so many things to say and thought I had a clear idea of the pattern the semester was taking. After the first paper and the discussion that died, though, I went back and carefully reread my piece. Something was going on in my classroom that was far different from the rosy, happy picture I had prematurely painted. I did something I had never done before. I wrote to the journal's editor and withdrew the article. Whatever I had to conclude about my returning to the classroom, it had to be honest, and what I had written was not.

This was a new ball game.

4

CONFLICT OF VALUES

Unchallenged kids get the message. If adults expect little of them, expect that they must be reminded, hectored, hassled, expect them to be goof-offs, then they will goof off. Of course, some people will goof off no matter what expectations are set. But teachers should assume the highest standard of performance until they are shown that it is not forthcoming.
—Theodore R. Sizer, *Horace's Hope* (1996, p. 89)

Despite the cohort nature of this group, looking back it is clear that they were not a happy or unified class, and I was not perceptive enough to see it quickly and clearly. Large-group discussions are something I conduct successfully all the time but, as a whole, this class did not discuss well or productively; what mattered most to them was launching their own points to me and in front of others but not really attending to what their classmates said. I encouraged cross-comments and comments on comments, but the students weren't buying it. Most times they either fell silent or mocked each other's comments. Using their journal writing to jumpstart the discussion worked, but it never seemed to work sufficiently. A different configuration was not the perfect answer, either: In small groups, despite my work with different sets of students, the cliques ruled.

Also, my blithe assumption that, yes, they had been working in revision groups and understood those parameters was short-sighted. It became apparent that the students did not know what to do when it came to helping each other with aspects of the assignments, and their interactions with group members were not always helpful. Yet I do believe that their lack of attention to the task could have been remedied if their teacher had had the good sense to trust what she was seeing and not what the students were saying. This was a true failure on my part, and, in hindsight, almost inexplicable. Without any kind of ability to interact productively in discussion and small groups, much of the work in small groups became a problem, and I did not intervene effectively.

WHAT HAPPENED TO THE WORK ETHIC?

There were certainly promising beginnings, but the student work ethic for this designated special, honors group continued to be a real surprise. I had not thought the issue would be such a large one, but it turned out to be huge. It came in two varieties: communication issues and absentee rate.

As with the first essay, when big assignments were due, many students just did not come to class. They always had signed excuses from their parents that the administration routinely honored, so there was no penalty for late work. According to Live Oak school regulations, any student whose parent signed an excuse (and they all did) had *six* school days to complete any assignment. About 30% of the class would be absent on due dates, and further, students would promise work and assignments that were not submitted. It was uncanny how many computers and printers at home broke the very night before an assignment was due, or how many disks containing precious final drafts were corrupted and would not open the next day in the school computer lab. Homework was definitely completed—*definitely completed*, students noted emphatically—but was somehow left on desks at home. Assignments, which had been sent to me by e-mail (*You didn't get it, Dr. C?*), apparently got lost in cyberspace. The class's deadlines were listed on the syllabus, a copy of which every student had in his or her class notebook, on the electronic bulletin board, on the classroom white board, and announced by myself on a daily basis: I was determined to be explicit about everything. Yet during every class two or three students —and not always the same students—remained perennially surprised about when things were due. For some students, the pattern was consistent: promises to bring in makeup work were somehow forgotten; conversations about deadlines were misinterpreted.

This was an aspect of student culture that I had not anticipated. For these students, the class and its requirements were obviously just one of many demands on their time: The distractions of other entertainments were everywhere, and somehow ditching an assignment or a class hardly seemed a large issue. When absent from class or coming to class empty-handed, no student even feigned real chagrin; that was essentially that. There was nothing about the school's culture that seemed to dictate a different attitude, and I was not going to be able to turn this around quickly. What mattered was not necessarily this one class.

One student could not get her deadlines straight: My phone call home to her mother, which I thought went cordially, upset her so much, she reported the next day, that she was unable to finish her assignment. It got complicated; Latosha was my weakest student, and I worried intensely about her ability to pass the class. After two weeks of back and forth, communication was at a nadir: I would tell Latosha one thing, and she would look at me blankly and ask a question that clearly indicated that she either did not understand or did not want to respond to what I was saying. She asked for private conferences during class, something I could not honor then and there. But my request for her to stay a minute after class to talk never worked: The bell rang, Latosha picked up her books, and she was history. Then Latosha started writing notes to me, and it became even murkier ("My computer broke down and was unable to print. It didn't take my disk. Do to this inconvenience, I have my Essay written on paper"). I never, however, received any essay, handwritten or typed, and it was getting serious. To clear things up and in some desperation, I ended up writing her a formal letter, trying to get it all straight. Looking back, it was most likely overkill, a detailed, legalistic memo written to a kid who was just offtrack. But after weeks of misunderstanding, it seemed so important at the time. I wrote Latosha:

> As you know, on February 24 you received an "R" (Revise) on Essay #1 with written comments as to what you were to do to revise the essay. I told you at the time that you could revise this within the nine weeks period, and I encouraged you twice to send me a pre-revision so that I could go over it before you submitted the final draft. I have not received anything from you to date. Once again, I urge you to follow my comments and to revise the paper.

You did not turn in Essay #2 on March 4 and asked for an extension. Upon my request, you did give me on March 4 a partial rough draft. On March 6 I returned this to you with comments. To date, though, I do not have the final version of Essay #2.

On March 6 you also handed me a note, signed by yourself and your mother, indicating that your computer was broken and that you would be finishing your essay during period 4 and giving it to your last semester's teacher to give to me. In a p.s.— which I assume was written after your mother signed the original note—you asked if you could submit the essay to me the next class. As I told you at the time, you have an open deadline to submit a revision of Essay #1. I also asked you to stay after class so that we could talk about this—I was not sure which alternative you were asking for or if you were referring to Essay #2—but you left when the bell rang.

You did not give a finished essay to last semester's teacher after period 4. Today I have neither a revision for Essay #1 nor a final draft for Essay #2.

You have repeatedly told myself and your other teachers— at times with tears—that you want to know what you can do to improve. We all want you to succeed, but you are not following through with assignments, with deadlines, and with what you say you will do.

If this is not clear, I will be happy to meet with you and with you and your parents.

Latosha did not come to talk, did not complete the essays, and I never heard from her mother again.

I came to feel like an Old Testament prophet who surveys the feckless misbehavior of the tribes and wants to condemn. It seemed from my perspective that the students wanted praise and wanted to have fun in class but really and truly did not want to do the extent of work required. In all my planning, considering that this was a "special" class carrying honors credit, this is one thing I had somehow missed: students for whom the work did not matter. I needed to recognize that if students could not manage deadlines and complete assignments, they would never work smoothly as a class. Further, I was beginning to feel the strain: I was stretching myself to do this thoroughly and well, working under the assumption that they were exceptional students, eager, and talented. What I was seeing, however, was something different. Regarding assignments and deadlines, they said they didn't hear it, didn't know it, hadn't been taught it before. Heavens.

Why oh why did I think these students were enormously competent and hardworking? Silly me—the absentee rate was approximately one-third whenever an assignment was due, and student promises, of e-mails, drafts, materials for class enrichment, were all pledged and never delivered. It extended to the very personal: Standing at the door at the beginning of class to greet students had always been important to me. It was a small thing but, again, greeting the students as they came in gave me an opportunity to interact just a bit, and to set a tone for the class to follow. But for this group, the practice seemed not to mean much at all. Most students appeared to barely notice I was there and seemed indifferent to my greeting or smiles; some just pushed on by. I was less miffed by this than curious: Was I, were many teachers, that invisible?

LOOKING FOR ADVICE

About five weeks into the semester, I decided to register formal alarm about what was happening regarding attendance, deadlines, and performance, and turned to both Terry and Kasey for serious advice. The first nine weeks' grades were looming, and I was worried about the students' work. In all our conversations the two were supportive, and their responses were both pragmatic and to the point. In one e-mail exchange, Terry noted that "I am really embarrassed of these students' behavior . . . it's inexcusable." Kasey's response, a snapshot of reality, came from her experience in her own class with the 22:

> For the most part, what you've described is the basic pattern of this group. About half are fine while there are various problems with the other half. . . . The same stuff is happening in [my] digital video class—I had about half turn in a project, the other

half is still deciding if they're going to do it. I drop a letter grade each late day. We're getting into negative numbers.

There is also a certain attitude with the group because they have been together for three years and they are the first media literacy class. Because of the nature of the . . . class . . . they are allowed to do things other students are not. These things make them feel like the rules don't apply to them.

Although there will always be someone absent in any given class, skipping is new this year because they now have cars and driver's licenses. Other than daily participation grades it's hard to get them because they have excused notes from their parents.

All of this is to say that I don't have any answers and that you've covered yourself with clear expectations of due dates and assignments. I may be able to help with . . . dealing with individual kids if you want. I'll come down for lunch tomorrow so we can compare notes.

We did compare notes, and, other than the sense of being in this together, there seemed to be no magic bullet, no wild innovation that would get the students back on track. At the end of the first nine weeks, only one student received an A. Eleven received Bs, but there were six Cs, one D, and a dismal three Fs.

THE FAILED LURE OF CHOICE

A major assumption I made about the students had to do with choice: I have always believed that if students—all students—are given options, they will be far more willing to do activities and to do well than otherwise. I practiced this in my earlier high school teaching, and I preach it in teacher education. So, in this class, choice was everywhere. There were set school district curriculum issues and topics (such as the required research paper) and pieces of literature (American lit and a range of canonical pieces in that area) but, within them, an array of choice: choices for journal entries, choices from six different American short stories, choices from five different research paper project topics (all of which had choices within choices), choices of three different young adult novels, and choices regarding the culminating projects for the novels. Students could work alone, in pairs, or in small groups. Student choice determined all vocabulary content and test questions. Within final tests, students had further choices of specific questions and essay questions, almost all of which had been originally created by them in small groups and shared with everyone.

During this experience, though, choice did not seem powerful. My students did not, I conclude, seem interested much in their choices: They took them as given, and the assignments as, once again, school assignments. The act of making a decision to do this instead of that, read this instead of that, was not any kind of panacea or, in some cases, even inducement. Choice, for this group, rarely meant responsibility. This was just school—choice was not any lure. This bedrock attitude could not be easily dislodged, and it made a menu of choices virtually meaningless.

For me, spontaneity began to wither; before class I had to remind myself to smile, praise, and laugh. It was clear that many of the students were not engaged by the class, many had no intention of taking responsibility for the kind of work I expected, and now that the novelty of a new teacher was past, they were ready to resume whatever they had previously defined as business as usual.

If that were not bad enough, my decision to create everything new (no textbooks, none of my prior materials or assignments adapted or reused, everything created for this class only) and to aggressively use student choice and student suggestion was time-consuming. Further, I was determined to post everything on the electronic site, to use all the strategies I thought were important, to respond and conference and communicate quickly and continuously, and it all made the experience at times overwhelming. I worked as hard on this course as I have ever worked, and when the response from the majority of students was virtually flat, it seemed almost a cruel joke.

PLANNING AND KEEPING TRACK

Long-range planning in most school settings is difficult, often next to impossible, and it is a focus of many reform efforts. From my perspective,

however, little has changed in this area, and it was particularly instructive to write and distribute to the students a syllabus for the first nine
weeks, only to revamp it almost entirely a total of three times, each time
reprinting it and distributing it and reposting it on the Live Oak electronic bulletin board. As when I taught high school decades ago, the
unexpected was everywhere: snow days, a guidance counselor visit
that lasted twice its projected time, a school opening delay and shorter
periods due to ice and sleet, two reschedulings of the state standardized tests, a last-minute disaster drill, a mandatory music concert. All
conspired to change my plans. Then, of course, there was the real need
to be responsive to students: There were absences of many members
of the class due to field trips, absences due to other class projects that
took students away, requests for extensions of deadlines. Flexibility is
important, and I responded accordingly. But although I know all of
this and teach it and workshop it with my secondary English methods
students, it was, nevertheless, tough to live it, deal with it, and repeatedly have to adjust.

Keeping up with the details and detritus of the classroom was another issue. It was truly time-consuming to track excused and unexcused
absences, parental calls for mid–marking period failing grades, and daily
posting of information and assignments on the electronic bulletin board.
As an outsider and a newcomer, I was careful about making mistakes: I
absolutely needed to know who was absent, who was tardy, who had
an extension to finish an assignment, who had not been in class for a
week. The student who had recently delivered her baby needed all her
work written out and sent to her homebound teacher; my student with
the IEP required additional assistance. Students who worked on media
projects in Kasey's class were generally allowed to be excused early, and
these students changed from day to day. My student with diabetes had
to leave every class 10 minutes early to have her blood sugar checked,
and there were others who came in and out due to clubs, field trips, and
excused trips with parents.

This is the nature of the comprehensive high school. This class, a
class I cherished, planned, and labored over, was subject to change at
little notice. And, as the semester went on, it was clear that I was probably one of the few who really worried about that. For the students, it
seemed the territory of low expectations, the land of little apparent

consequence. Work could be made up or not; parental excuses in this school district mandated that absences were always excused and always gave students days and days to complete missing or late assignments. Schedules? Deadlines? It was a nonissue for students. And I could not let go enough to make it a nonissue for me.

What was happening, in hindsight, was what I caution my teacher preparation students against all the time: letting the plan dictate the teaching and becoming so involved with keeping on schedule—however laudable the schedule may be—that you lose sight of the reality of the classroom. All I knew and felt was that the crafted, intricate curriculum I had negotiated with the students, in which I was so interested and pleased, was being eroded on a daily basis. For me, that represented not a challenge to change but a defeat. Even after all these years of teaching, my wisdom about students and school seemed insufficient to save me from myself.

And then came the most intricate project of the semester: the research paper.

5

WHEN A PROJECT GOES BAD

The research paper, commonly known as going to the [web] and expanding.
—Beth Hagy, student, in Leila Christenbury,
Making the Journey (2006, p. 233)

One of the major criticisms of the American comprehensive high school is the shallow approach to sustained intellectual engagement. Projects are not extensive, writing and research is neglected. An antidote to this concern is the research paper, which can offer students real possibility of engagement. On the other hand, the research paper can also be a barrier to students. Thus, the research paper frets me. It is a staple in English language curriculum although it is fraught with even more difficulties and challenges than it was when I first was in the high school classroom. Although the "you'll need this for college" mantra still persists, the research paper has become so institutionalized in many school districts that the gathering of information and the making of resource lists and notes has often come to overbalance the actual writing of the paper itself: Incredibly, some districts never even ask students to finish a final draft. What has complicated the issue, of course, is the Internet; my student Beth Hagy's comment about going there and expanding is a reality. With Web sites that can be disguised as original research, with a wealth of free papers and even for-fee papers on the Internet, an original research paper is a tough sell.

Writing about the research paper in the high school classroom, I have many ideas about its implementation. Years before I returned to high school teaching, I observed in *Making the Journey* (2000):

Most students hate this assignment; most teachers dread not just the difficulty of getting students through the process but the lifeless results of what seem to be hours of preparation. Further, plagiarism is a serious issue in the research paper, and my very brief advice is to give students an opportunity to write about something in which they are interested . . . letting students pursue in their research something they want to search out. Certainly we need to remember that primary and secondary research can be done on an amazing range of subjects. It is not just the Romantic Movement in England in the early 1800s or the use of fire imagery in a novel that should be the sole subject of student investigation. Certainly there are students in your English language arts class who may want to research Bret Harte's short stories or Toni Morrison's metaphors. But there are those who can also do excellent jobs researching the history of their neighborhood, the latest innovations in four-wheel-drive technology, the newest theories on the planets, or the influence of the Industrial Revolution on just about everything. (p. 241)

And this is just what I tried to do when I returned to the high school classroom, having my students, though their Images of America/Coming to America curriculum, choose a huge variety of topics.

THE GREAT RESEARCH PAPER PLAN

What could they do? I gave them multiple options (see Appendix A for the full assignment). Along with the option of choosing any topic, I also suggested five other possible research topics they could explore:

- *Family History*, where students could use primary sources such as interviews with family members; family documents such as baby books, recipes, photographs, and letters; and could include autobiographical incidents and anecdotes, information on special family celebrations, maxims and proverbs, foods, distinct family experience and behavior, and sketches of various family members. The paper could also touch on the broader ethnic literature of the family, including folk tales, myths and legends, proverbs, historical fiction, nonfiction, films.
- *Date of Birth*, where a student could take his or her birthday, taking it as the starting point and focus and research that day from a number of perspectives, that of the family, the community where they were born, the nation, and the world.

- *Any American author* of fiction, nonfiction, or poetry (or a jour-nalist or humorist) with an overview of the author's work, the ideas and themes the writer addressed, and what might be im-portant about reading this writer today.
- *Themes in American literature*, what makes this theme appealing or important to American literature and to what extent we learn about it from the literature and to what extent the theme is being addressed today.
- *American cultural touchstone* and its history, origins, use, and marketing (cultural touchstones could be a number of topics such as baseball, Coca-Cola, motorcycles, rap and hip-hop, the ham-burger, suburbia, the summer vacation, the cookout, Thanksgiv-ing, the car, our national park system, the interstate highway).

I was trying to replicate my own advice that I had given teachers in a previous book, advice that governed my philosophy of what the re-search paper could be and how it could be successfully implemented:

> If teachers follow the kinds of guidelines listed above, students can broaden the idea of what research actually means, concluding that research sources can come from many areas. It is not just journal articles, books, and even information from Internet searches that can constitute quotable and use-able research sources. Also, when we give students a platform to display their findings—such as in a discussion forum and through publication— we reinforce the fact that research is more about finding answers and pursing ideas than fulfilling some kind of disembodied English teacher assignment. . . . One caveat I would add to these many ideas about re-search projects is that it is a teacher's responsibility, if there are multiple parts to a research paper assignment, to set up an incremental system so that students can not only keep track of what they are doing but also gar-ner points along the way. Thus, you might give students an assignment sheet with the following kind of deadlines and progressive credit. Both of these, the deadlines and the point credit, will help keep students on track and give them a sense of progress in their project and in their final grade. (*Making the Journey*, 2000, p. 242)

Using my own published, hypothetical, eight-week schedule for a stu-dent research projects, which includes topic and source work, individual conferences, revision groups, and three drafts, two of which are handled in student revision groups, I set up with my Live Oak students an exact and detailed schedule (see Appendix A).

I discussed this with the students, and although many of them claimed never to have heard of those strange things called "citations," Kasey assured me that she had spent two weeks the previous year on source citation. Accordingly, I gave students a brief review, and thanks to the Live Oak librarians, there was a handy Web site where sources could be put into proper form. As a class, we talked about topics and ideas and what the students might be interested in. Early on, we went to the library to find out about the sources for their varying topics, and although no one seemed to listen closely to the librarian's careful explanation and her demonstration of what she had preloaded for the class onto the Live Oak Web site, I assumed that inattention was not particularly important. Back in class, I told students that although this project was required by the school system, I was really hoping that whatever they chose would be of real interest to them.

When students chose their topics, I placed their names and ideas on the electronic bulletin board and on a bulletin board in the classroom: It seemed to me that students who did similar projects—family histories or touchstones in America or the date of their birth—would want to consult with each other, and when we were in revision groups, research topic choice also dictated the composition of the group.

It was consistent with what I thought a research paper could be and with what I had advised other teachers to do. It all seemed well-thought-out—at least to me.

PARENTS ARE NOT ALWAYS OUR FRIENDS

When I first taught high school, the parents of my students were tired. They were working two jobs, they mistrusted the school (largely due to community racial tensions, some of which were long-standing), and the upshot was that I saw few of them during the year. Further, few of the students I taught years ago were harmonious with their parents—the clashes and misunderstandings were often reported in my hearing, and in general, parents were not seen as positive forces in most of my students' lives. I was under no illusion that that scenario was viable in this setting, and I had heard previous stories from Terry and Kasey of parental upsets and arguments and confrontations between teachers and parents during the previous semesters. Parents in this school setting were active advocates for their children, and the students were prepared and willing to bring their parents into classroom- and teacher-related issues. I felt I had been warned.

My first encounter with a parent was, however, positive. Neal's mother felt I was the first and only teacher who had encouraged her son. Although I did not think that was accurate, I took the praise and appreciated it. After that event, however, there were few positive encounters.

Alex was a sweet and kind young man who did absolutely nothing in class. When he chose to share a journal entry or speak, it was clear he was smart, but, like Bartleby, he preferred not. I called Alex's parents, and his mother patiently heard my spiel about his obvious intelligence and dismal work habits, but then said she had had teachers tell her this for years. She told me she was tired of being informed that Alex was smart and was aware that he did not work in class. If I couldn't come up with a solution, what was she to do? As far as she was concerned, I was bringing nothing to the table. Case closed. She hung up the phone.

I lost Ellen Patton when I noted that she might want to use spell-check and that a dozen or more usage errors in a final draft had to be acknowledged and penalized. Ellen was not amused. Once she received her essay, graded and with my comments, her mood shifted markedly and for the rest of the class, she would not participate or even look at me. She left the class telling her friends loudly enough for me to overhear that she had never before received a B.

The Shadow of Plagiarism

Thus when, on rough draft #1 of her research paper I reminded Ellen to cite sources, the door was evidently opened for full warfare. I had, it seemed, not asked Ellen to check sources but had accused her of cheating; she was emotionally devastated, and her divorced parents found a common ground, finally, to unite.

It was byzantine: I received an e-mail from my host teacher, Terry, who had talked to Kasey, the department chair of Media Literacy, who had been informed by the English Department chair, yet another person, who had called her because Mr. Patton had called Ms. Wood the principal and wanted a meeting. How the other chair was involved, I had no idea; despite my posted e-mail address, phone numbers, and electronic bulletin board, no one contacted me and, when I talked to Ellen one-on-one, she simply got quiet on the phone and told me nothing was wrong: How did I get that idea? But something was wrong, and what ensued was a weekend round of telephone calls to and from: Mrs. Patton, Mr. Patton, Mr. Patton about Mrs. Patton, Ellen Patton, Terry, Kasey, Ellen again, and then resolution.

I mentioned the research paper, the research paper handout, and the class discussion of plagiarism, the function of rough drafts, and my function as a responsible teacher to ask about citations before citations became serious and possibly erroneous, even plagiaristic. Live Oak High School's published regulations indicated a stiff stand on plagiarism, and provided, in the school handbook, a suggested punishment of a zero on plagiarized assignments, a parent notification, and two days of suspension for intentional—or unintentional—"copying or imitating of the language and ideas of another and claiming them as one's own." It seemed pretty straightforward to me but, for sure, not to the students and not to their parents. The whole incident took an enormous amount of time but, by Monday morning, all parties seemed to understand why I had had the temerity to ask Ellen to check her citations.

Ellen's final paper, scanned by turnitin.com, was clean, but the damage was permanent. After the research paper was over, Ellen nursed a sense of grievance that she never got over the entire class. She did not meet my eyes in class, did not volunteer, would not participate in any large-group discussions, although once she did allow that the sample movie trailers I had used were inadequate and she had better ones at home, which she volunteered to bring in—and of course never did.

And the citation issue didn't end there. Another Ellen in class, Ellen Walls, wrote an e-mail saying that although she had not cited any sources in her rough draft, and I had alerted her to that necessity, some-how that alert was not a good thing at all. Invoking the power of the group, she wrote:

> It was kind of disheartening and I, along with some other classmates, felt as if you believed that we'd actually be dishon-est to plagiarize by stealing someone elses ideas! It's unfortu-nate and disappointing when some people actually research and took time out to write their paper, but are accused of allegedly cheating. Believe me, there are no hard feelings, I just wanted you to know how I, am some other classmates, felt before we turned in our final draft.

But the two Ellens were just the tip of the iceberg.

The Excused Absence Phenomenon

To come were the five students who did not turn in their research paper rough draft #2—a draft that needed to be turned in on time because I needed to respond to it, give it the agreed-upon completion points, and get it back to the students asap. Time was tight: The final draft was due the next week, and I was off to a previously scheduled and completely unavoidable professional meeting. I needed rough draft #2 on time to be able to help students with their revisions. So what to do with the students who, as usual, cut class the day the rough draft was due? They could not get my feedback—I had stayed in the library for two hours after class to write comments on what I had just received from the stu-dents, and made sure that they had the papers back that very day. I then drove straight to the airport. For the students who cut class that day, there were no drafts and, therefore, no comments from me and, of course, no completion points.

And then the parents—though different parents—came out again.

Yes, Erin took the day off and didn't turn in her rough draft #2—but Erin's mother was emphatic that there were very "personal" rea-sons why Erin not only was not in school but did not do the work, and she was going to the principal Ms. Wood immediately to protest the lost points. School policy dictated that students had six class days to

complete "missed work," and despite my careful research paper schedule, a draft was nothing more than missed work—Erin could turn in
the draft, technically, when the rest of the class was through with the
entire paper. The rumor mill had told me the real story and, sure enough,
Erin's mother later on admitted that Erin took the day off to be with her
long-distance boyfriend who was unexpectedly in town. Her mother
wanted Erin and her boyfriend to be together, and that was that.

Karol's mother also wrote an e-mail that noted she was "very angry"
about the lost points: Although Karol was not in class and did not
e-mail her draft or send it in with a classmate, "it is totally unfair of
you to penalize a conscientious student like Karol." The mother knew
the school regulations well:

> It is also unheard of that you are going against the school's
> policy for make-up work with an excused absence. . . . I intend
> to talk with the principal and anyone else that I need to get this
> situation made right. My daughter is an excellent student and
> does not deserve this.

The upshot with other students was that, yes, a number of the students
just didn't have the rough draft. But so what—the comments were
obviously dispensable, but the students needed the points. The draft
was nothing more than "missed work," students had six school days
to complete it, and somehow my carefully designed research paper
schedule, giving points for each segment, was not foolproof against
student and parental protest or against excused absences that meant
extension after extension after extension.

I was caught, in this issue and in others, in a legalistic quagmire.
Regarding the research paper, what hadn't I said? Looking back on it,
many things, and the specter of the parents, the students' absences, all
highlighted it. I hadn't written out each segment in detail: that the first
draft must be a draft, not the first two pages of a Web site (Sharon
taught me that lesson); that the second draft must be different from
the first (this revelation came from Susan); that the total absence of a
bibliography would result in a failing grade for the research paper (when
Latosha's promised bibliography did not materialize, my own evaluation percentages did not allow me to take the appropriate draconian

action). I hadn't written that the drafts must be turned in on time in order to function as drafts (about one-third of the class taught me this); that the question of sources is not an accusation but a help (Ellen Patton and Ellen Walls and others, this lesson is from you).

It was a train wreck. I created part of it, school regulations contributed their share, the students took advantage of almost everything they could, and it took time and time and time to fix.

THE RESEARCH PAPER RESULTS

In the end, though, it was also oddly successful. I talked to all of the concerned parents and explained the citation/plagiarism issue, noting that the school district itself was alarmed by the practice of downloading papers from the Internet. Karol's mother apologized and noted that rereading her own e-mail, she thought she may have been rude (yes, she was, but I saw no point in telling her so), and the other parents seemed to be mollified. As for the students, who presented their papers in two days of class, the project seemed to resonate.

The day the final papers were due, we did a panel presentation in class. This seemed to be something the students had never done, and they responded. Those who did family histories came to the front of the class to present; later, those who researched aspects of American culture or American writers followed them. Finally came those who had researched just what was going on in the world and the community on the day they were born. I was the impromptu emcee, using a prop to simulate a microphone, asking questions, cheering the audience on. It was a cross between Oprah and Maury Povich, and for once the class actually listened as others discussed what they had found and what meant something to them. This mattered.

Especially for students who researched their family history, the paper was emotional and powerful. Helen came with real artifacts from her grandmother's trunk, which she passed around for the class to handle and touch—a powder horn a relative had used in the Revolutionary War and a Civil War canteen. Certainly Helen may have been a bit overly proud of what she had discovered as family aristocratic roots—incurring the disdain of some of her classmates—but she also

talked frankly during her paper presentation about how she had un-
covered that a number of her relatives had been members of the Ku
Klux Klan, and she was shocked and angered by that fact. The resulting class discussion on racism, historical and contemporary, was the
first of its kind for the semester. For Jackie, interviewing her grand-
father, who had immigrated to this country in the 1940s, was a revelation. Much of what she shared in her presentation was also in an
impassioned e-mail she sent me:

> I know it is late and I do not know when you will get this . . .
> but I had to talk to you. Tonight I went to my Papou's house. It
> was the first day since him and my grandmother have been
> back from Greece (before I have been getting all information
> over telephone, so it has been hard.) But tonight, was the first
> night I sat down with him, with a tape recorder and listened, for
> about 5 hours. And to tell you, my PaPoule never likes to speak
> of the past very much, so I have never herd many stories of his
> life. I cried Dr. Cristeanbury. I never knew my grandfather was
> such an amazing man. He spoke tonight of his studies in Chem-
> istry in Germany during the rise of Hitler and persecution of the
> Jews, fighting as a Lieutenant in the Greek Army in W.W. II, all
> the battles and hardships he faced, loosing his brother in the
> war, the family's industry loosing its factory after the Marshall
> Plan, and then him coming here, he invented a chemical called
> Esther that is in Dove soap. Honestly, I was dumbfounded. I
> know I am rambling, but I am so excited about this paper now,
> and my heart and soul will go into writing it. I have never felt
> so proud to be his granddaughter. And I also wanted to thank
> you for telling me to record the conversations because now I
> will cherish that for life, it's honestly a conversation I will never
> forget. . . . Thank you for giving me this assignment.

Neal, my bright dysgraphic, also wrote me a note: "I decided to
weight you this letter to let you know a few things that are on my mind.
For starters I wanted to tell you how much I enjoyed wrighting this
paper it gave me the chance to find things out about my family that I
had never knew."

Other students investigated their birth dates and those who chose American writers or culture researched Hollywood, blue jeans, blues music, fast food, Kurt Vonnegut, Fredrick Douglass, the Harlem Renaissance, the young adult writer Annette Klaus, and the Beat poets. Much of the work was solid and interesting. The final grades were largely in the A and B range, and no one plagiarized.

Was it worth it? Teachers don't usually think of projects in these terms, but this project was a strain for me. Yes, some of it was worth it. Mostly, thank heavens, it was over. What the research paper also showed, however, was how the combination of school regulations, student attitude, and parental intervention could make such a project harrowing for a teacher. Values were not in synch, and, in some ways, it was a project gone bad.

6

THE STRUGGLE FOR ENGAGEMENT

Only connect.
—E. M. Forster, *Howard's End* (Chapter 22, 1910/1997)

E. M. Forster's two-word admonition stands as a landmark in literary exhortations, and it's good advice for the classroom, too. Connecting with, caring about, engaging, making bridges of meaning with students, is essential for a productive classroom. The basics of connection often lie in classroom setup: Students and teachers need to feel a sense of community, shared enterprise, and even mutual regard. Although not every period has to be a lovefest, it helps immensely when students and teachers feel a sense of care and connection.

For me, one major connective piece of tissue is the subject matter itself; belief in its utility can be the important link in the classroom. When for students, however, it does not matter, the personal engagement becomes even more important. I made some of those connections in my return to high school teaching, but not as many as I needed. Due to a paper assignment and discussion that did not go as she wanted, Alice came to mistrust me early in the semester; Ellen Patton felt I did not give her sufficient praise or trust her integrity; Latosha would not respond to direction, questions, or comments. But for some others, a positive bond was established.

STUDENTS WITH WHOM I CONNECTED

I connected quickly with Neal through my response to his strong journal entries, and he decided early on that I was the best English teacher he had ever had. His mother had written me an e-mail saying I had changed his whole attitude ("you have been able to do something no one ever had and that is get him really interested in English"). Later Neal wrote:

> I also wanted to tell you how much I am enjoying your class when we were told that you a college professor was going to come in to be our teacher for the second semester I was a little scarred thinking that you would be supper hard. But I was wrong you are hard but not as hard as I was thinking. . . . There is one more thing that I would like to tell. I would like to tell you thank you for every thing that you have done for me also want to thank you for being so understanding of my disabilities in writing.

My new student mother, Sharonda, wrote me what I thought was a brave and forthright note just days after her delivery regarding her determination to succeed in the class and finish all of her assignments. I was honored to get this and told her so.

Emma was funny, hysterical, witty in her journal entries and adult-like serious about her inability to meet a deadline. She earnestly promised to improve, understood fully that she was having trouble making the clock and her schedule work together, and was just a bright shiny penny in the class. She made me laugh, and I loved her for that.

Ashton was one of the best writers I had ever seen in high school and along with her friends in the class, Karol and Mary, could always be counted on to produce good work and on time. The three were not strong social forces in class discussion, but their presence and consistency were often comforting.

Starr was a dreamy, creative, quiet student, whose watchful eyes and shy smiles let me know, again and again and again, that she got it, she understood, and she would do something brilliant with it. She did, and did frequently. She was the one student who always dressed in a different style from the rest of the group, a little punkish, a little sixties mod. She always was the student who would work with the two weakest members of the class, Latosha and Susan, and seemed never to worry that her popularity or prestige might be affected by her stance. Starr truly moved to her own, unheard music. In fact, I finally realized how I "remembered" her—she reminded me strongly of an article (Bassett, 1998)

I published when I was editor of *English Journal*, "An English Class with Emily," where teacher Lawrence Bassett observes with awe:

> But now it's first period, we're talking about *The Scarlet Letter*, and I'm grateful that it's a quiet talk so close to a vacation. . . . It's so quiet that I have to call on someone, and Emily is it, and I watch, spellbound, as she looks off into some distant space, up toward the lights somewhere, where she can see her soul suspended among the fluorescent tubes, and I listen, entranced, as she says, hesitantly at first, trying to fit words to the illuminations that she sees and the imminences that she feels, "I like Hester."
>
> That's all. She likes Hester.
>
> "I like Hester because she's strong . . . I wanted to be strong, and I wasn't. I didn't know how. But now," she says, "now I do." She's looking up, looking out instead of inward. "Now I do," she says. "I can be like Hester." (pp. 64–65)

Starr seemed to me to be like Bassett's Emily. Her eclectic dress, unlike anyone in the class; her quiet and watchful ways; her constant ability to both stand alone—a member of no clique—and yet to always go into pairs or groups with those who were weaker academically; these qualities made her powerful to me. I would find myself checking Starr's face and find her watching me; she often smiled shyly during class as if there was a secret joke or connection. As the semester went on, I came to feel there was.

But Starr was elusive, as are many students. She did not stay after class to talk with me, did not ask my opinion or advice, did not want me to linger at her desk when I was making the class rounds. She simply inhabited Trailer 11 and was, I think, not only an academic force but, in many ways for me, a spiritual one. When Starr's eyes lit up in class, it was a good day.

Anthony became a challenge for me. He would not commit to a research paper topic, and after some prodding—and loss of points as he missed the deadline—settled on the mullet as his focus. I needed clarification—which I wrote him and also asked him one-on-one. Evidently, my query seemed so bogus to him—of course it wasn't the fish, it was the haircut—that he would not respond to me; and that was not, I thought, a responsible and useful posture. Things deteriorated after that, and we clashed; to be vulgar about it, he was a smart ass, I was a hard ass. Despite his excellent grasp of vocabulary—he routinely made the highest grades of anyone in the class, and I noted that repeatedly and with unfeigned admiration—he would not communicate regarding other assignments, and I was unwilling to keep asking and asking and asking. Then his father suffered trauma in an industrial accident, falling 14 feet off a ladder and ending up with brain injuries. Anthony was upset on a number of levels; his parents were divorced, and he had chosen to live with his more accommodating father. It looked like he would have to return home to live with his mother. I talked to his mother and also to Anthony. I told him, honestly, that some of our difficulty was his fault, but for sure some was mine, too. I asked about his father. And then we were better. His father recovered, and Anthony went on to finish the class with his usual high grades. There were no more clashes.

For some reason, from almost the beginning of the semester, Lee acted as if she almost loved me, and from the first she wanted my approval, comments, and interaction. She came in early to class and stayed late, wanting to share her ideas or observations. Shy, unpopular with other students in the class, and hesitant, she was feeling her way in high school. I tried to acknowledge her and give her some time. Halfway through the semester she wrote me an unexpected note:

> I just wanted to say thinks for coming in this semester. I believe this was a great opportunity for a college professor to come and teach us. You certainly broke the sterotype of a professor. I mean that in a nice way. You are one of the most caring teachers I've met and that mans a lot to me. I will truly miss you next year. If you have time, just stop by say hi. I'd like that.

I liked that, too.

THE STUDENT WHO WOULDN'T—
AND THEN WHO WOULD

Susan was a pleasant student but extremely quiet and self-effacing, one who would not share anything in large-group discussion and who, in small-group work, always paired with folks who seemed to be more energetic than she and could accomplish the work. At one point, she completely stopped writing in her journal, even though all of us were working on it during class. Previously she had written a strong entry on her father, a man who had ceased to be a part of her life some time ago and who, even on Christmas and her birthday, failed to acknowledge her presence. His new family seemed to be his focus, and it hurt Susan immensely. I talked with her during and after class—I, too, had had a difficult time with my father—but got almost nothing from her but averted eyes and mumbles. I checked with Terry, and there were rumors about Susan's health, her love life, all of which could have explained her lack of affect in school. There was an older boyfriend for whom she had, alarmingly, made two court appearances, but, despite all that and her indifference to work, she loved one particular large Deep South university and believed firmly that in a year or so she would escape high school and be a student there.

But Susan's work was so marginal and skimpy that when the second nine-week, midterm grades were given, I called her mother for the nth time. Susan's mother was one of the parents with whom I connected positively and strongly, and she appreciated my efforts to keep in touch. This crisis, however, was serious, and over the phone we plotted and planned and arranged for her to come to school where we would meet jointly with Susan. Perhaps the surprise of the two of us—making an impromptu intervention—would cause some change. Certainly Susan registered surprise when she was called to the office during first period, only to see both myself and her mother waiting for her, but the discussion the three of us had in the empty cafeteria did not seem earth-shattering. Susan had no answers and no reasons, and made no promises to do anything differently in class.

On the other hand, just a few weeks later, Susan chose a young adult novel, and the breakthrough appeared to come. She chose one of the creative projects, an ABC book, and put her phrases on construction paper, tied together with yarn. Susan had raided her mother's sewing kit to put on each page pearls, sparkles, beads, and all sorts of glitter. The content was not remarkable, the presentation was a bit messy, not professional at all, but the entire effect was wonderful, full and consistent with the spirit of the book itself. It was, in many ways, a triumph. I couldn't praise her enough.

Whether the discussion with Susan's mother had been the trick or not, it seemed to signal a shift in Susan, and she did pass the semester.

THE NOTE THAT WAS NOT
MEANT TO BE FOUND

Near the end of the semester, straightening up desks after the end of class, I found a packet that had fallen on the floor. It was folded and fat, and it looked like a note. I was curious—I opened it, read it. It was Latosha's distinctive, large, looping handwriting, and in it was detailed real fear and upset. Latosha had evidently sold candy as part of a school project and, like so many students, had spent the money, and now that the project had concluded, needed to repay it. But the consequences she foresaw were serious: She wrote in the note that she would need to contact X so that she could sell "stuff" (drugs) to get the money and that would be impossible because her mother was, once again, beating her, and the bruises were visible. Terry and I consulted; the guidance counselor and Latosha were put together for a discussion; the note was forwarded on. Latosha was her usual phlegmatic self—she made no reaction and issued no explanation, denials, or comments. I never knew precisely what happened in the end, but I hoped that Latosha's mother did indeed stop beating her and that she never got into temporary drug trafficking for her candy-money-spending. This was a dangerous and sad situation for Latosha, and it made me concerned for her, a concern that was divorced from our difficulty with deadlines and assignments. The incident was the closest any of my students at Live Oak had come to the real-world issues of my former high school years ago, and, in a way, it was oddly familiar territory.

ONLY CONNECT

Despite the good connections with some of my students, it was not universal. Mutuality is a delicate thing, and perhaps of all the characteristics of my Live Oak High School class of 22 students, that is what may have been lacking. Students initially thought that what we could do would be something like college but a lot more fun than what they perceived their other English classes to be. For my part, I initially thought that a rich, diverse high school course would tour students through an array of literature and writing and creative projects. This, for me, was the focus, and I think I underestimated the students and their needs and overestimated profoundly the power of the subject matter and its ability to make students care.

And the engineering of the rich, super–high school course may also have contributed to my lack of success. Looking back, it may all have been too much for everyone, and when the students felt overwhelmed, they did what many students will do: They resisted. The good news for me is that I was no unusual or hated target—Terry and Kasey had stories and stories of similar issues with members of the class—but it struck me especially hard, considering my expectations. My knowledge and ability regarding teaching strategies and a student-centered best practice was just not enough. Further, it all occurred in a short window of time, one semester, a semester that did not begin the school year. Finally, there was no chance to regroup and try again in future months.

It was also a far cry from the experience of one of my first-year English students, Lydia, who during her first year of teaching wrote to me of her progress. Lydia was an older student with children of her own who had returned to the university to finish her degree and become an English teacher. Like many of my students, she was hard-working and dogged; although she was not at the top of her class, she was determined. It would never have been my choice for her, but Lydia accepted her first teaching position at a tough middle school with a reputation for difficult students, some violence, and very low scores on the state standardized tests. The school personnel were under pressure, and there had been significant turnover in staff during the past few years. Lydia, one of the few Caucasian teachers in a largely African-American school, wrote an ecstatic, triumphant e-mail:

> I . . . can't wait to go back and start the New Year. Several of my students from last year have called or written me over the summer. They promise to visit me on the first day of school. I know they will. [The school] is indeed very rough and gang-like environment. There are fights and confrontations daily. Teachers

have had serious run-ins with students. I feel really bad for those teachers and students. I remember being told during teacher training that if you connect with your students, there is nothing they won't do for you. How true that is! I can say that I didn't have any discipline problems or instances that students disrespected me. In fact, my students would tell other students, "You better not disrespect her!" I really don't know what I did to receive this loyalty. My students would act up from time to time but never to the point of causing a confrontation with me. There were fights between other students happening outside my classroom and while other classrooms emptied to watch the fight, my students stayed focused on the lesson and did not leave their seats. I know it sounds fantastic and quite frankly I am surprised by it also. I would tell my students that they were wonderful, and I even called them nicknames such as "my precious ones," "my achievers," "my smart ones," etc. . . . silly names like that. They seemed to love it.

Indeed they did, and while I was so pleased for Lydia and wrote her my warmest response, I was wholly aware that that kind of bond is one I never had with almost any of my students at Live Oak. Although I had strong ties to Starr and Susan and Lee, although Neal thought I was a wonderful teacher, in my classroom there was nothing like what Lydia was experiencing. I could not motivate Alex, I could not make peace with Ellen Patton, and until the very end I could not get Susan to engage. Rereading Lydia's email, I remembered just who told her that "if you connect with your students there is nothing they won't do for you." This is something I knew, something I taught my own students, something Lydia heard directly from me, and something I could not achieve at Live Oak High School. The knowledge was hard to swallow.

7

THE STATE TEST:
UNINTENDED CONSEQUENCES

*Now, what I want is Facts. Teach these boys and girls nothing but Facts.
Facts alone are wanted in life. Plant nothing else, and root out everything
else.*

—Charles Dickens, *Hard Times* (1854/1965, p. 3)

The pressure of high-stakes testing has affected schooling at all levels, and the tests themselves can become all that matters to both teachers and students. In the middle of all my concern about my relationship to my students and about student response to deadlines and work ethic and how the class was going, came time for part one of the state standardized test. These high-stakes tests were administered in two parts, separated by a few weeks, during junior year in English, and their importance could not be exaggerated. At the end of the testing, all across the state, school and school district scores are made public, analyzed, and used to determine reward, transfer, and reputation for both administrators and teachers alike. For students, passing all of these tests also had a bearing on graduation and, in some districts, on whether students would be required to take year-end exams.

I was fully aware of this pressure. A few months before I began teaching, I met with Ms. Wood, Live Oak High School's principal. Having lived and worked in the area for almost 20 years, I was familiar with Ms. Wood professionally. My student teachers had been in the school for years, and I knew many of the English teachers; along with Kasey and Terry, a number of others had taken my courses. Despite this connection and my long history in education in the area, there was little personal warmth expended during our very brief meeting. Ms. Wood was polite but perfunctory and had only two things to note: She did not care what I did with the students during the spring semester or what I taught, but she did intensely care that they all pass both parts of the annual state English exam, administered that spring semester. With that, she stood, and the meeting was over. It had taken five minutes.

I saw Ms. Wood informally one other time during my teaching at Live Oak, but there were no further meetings or communication.

In many ways, those five minutes told me volumes about the current state of the American comprehensive high school and the pressures on it to meet regulations and test requirements. It was prescient in a way that I could not have anticipated and had real implications for what would happen to me and my students in the upcoming semester. But all I knew and cared about was that the teaching would soon start, and I could not wait to begin. I would deal with the test later. Although I have little quibble with my state's standards or with, frankly, most school district standards, I hate the required tests. On the other hand, my students needed to do well on this measure, with me or without me, and accordingly I shoved whatever reservations I might have had to the back of my mind and prepared to plow on.

REVIEWING FOR THE TEST

Consulting with Terry, I put together and duplicated a whole series of review materials, which the students and I could use not only for content review but also for a quick update on the vagaries of the multiple-choice question. Some of these came from old state tests, and some came from commercial sources. Whatever qualms I had I squelched: this was important beyond *me*, and I set aside two class periods—three hours— for this refresher course and review. For part one, we looked at sample test questions and, for part two, the writing portion, I worked up a pedestrian but practical handout (see Figure 7.1).

I had dreaded the two review days. Even though I was ready with a pep talk, some advice on standardized tests, and some planned rewards, the first day of review seemed doomed. An errant soccer ball had hit the side of Trailer 11, a window had been shattered, and while it was being repaired and the glass shards swept up, all of us had to

FIGURE 7.1. Review for SOL Writing Test: Sample Prompts

[Prompt is given in the form of a question, an issue, or a hypothetical "what-if" situation]

Essay Prompts

- In your opinion, what is the greatest challenge that teens face today?
- In your opinion, what is the biggest problem at your high school?
- What do you think of the idea that the minimum driving age would be raised to 18? Write an opinion piece for your school newspaper. Support your position with reasons and examples.
- What do you think is the best (or worst) advice you ever received? Why was it the best (or worst)? Be sure to explain and support your answer with reasons and examples.
- Discuss how an historical event from the past has affected your life, today.
- Imagine that you have been elected the chief advisor to President George W. Bush. This week, what would you advise him and why?
- How would your life change if you won a million dollars? Describe the specifics.

Persuasive Letter Prompts

- Some people feel that we need to bring back the draft. Write a letter to President Bush stating your position.
- Should teenagers be allowed to work as much as they want to during a week? Write a letter to one of our U.S. senators.
- What do you think of many public schools' policy of "zero tolerance"? Write a letter to the Martin County Board of Education and defend your position.

Purpose

To inform, explain, analyze, entertain,[*] persuade

Patterns of Organization

Chronological (tell a story,[*] describe events, explain a procedure)

Spatial (describe a layout, explain where something is located[*])

Cause and Effect (why an event or series or events occurred; tell about the result of or reason for the events)

Compare and Contrast (argue that one thing is better or worse than another)

Order of Importance (give reasons for holding a position and persuade reader of that position)

---

[*] Dr. C's best bet: unlikely on the test

move next door to a nearby vacant trailer which was, if such could be imagined, in even worse repair than ours. Many of the overhead lights in this trailer were burned out, there was a large hole in the floor which students needed to skirt as they walked in, and another hole in one side wall with insulation spilling out. All of us were perched in unfamiliar desks and in a shadowy, unfamiliar space.

The surprise, however, was how students reacted. They assembled in the neighboring trailer with little disruption, and after I made my comments and observations on tests and testing, got to work immediately. There was no extra talk and no complaining. Using the review materials, the students did silent work, pair work, and large-group work with numerous test items and did not interrupt each other or chat at all. They raised their hands; they were eager to participate. I was taken aback. This was the most focused they had been and the most traditionally well-behaved since the beginning of the year. It struck me that the students were geared for this, interested, and engaged. Evidently, this review and the upcoming test were real school stuff, and they seemed far less concerned than I about the trial to which they were being put. Apparently, this test really mattered, maybe even more than many of the activities we had done in class.

Obviously, students knew this territory well. They greeted the second day of review the same way and took part one of the test quietly and willingly. When they took part two of the test some time later and we prepared for it through review again, the attitude was similar. In some ways, it was clear that my Live Oak students were far more comfortable and at ease with the multiple-choice tests and the timed essay than with the discussion and writing that I asked them to do. This was real school, and the resistance and upset I anticipated was not evident. What did become evident, however, was that the state test could and did overshadow all other subsequent curricular concerns.

DIDN'T I GET THAT MEMO?

The two-part state test, with students' interest in the days of review and general acquiescence to the testing itself, also had other consequences that I had not anticipated at all. The week after the administration of part two, I thought LaBelle was kidding when she stood at her desk at the beginning of class, looked me in the eye, and told me that she would not be doing any more work for the rest of the semester because the state assessment tests were now completed. This was a student who wanted a college recommendation from me and who had been fairly steady in her work and attendance. But now, she said, the semester was *over*. Later in class, as I was introducing our next segment—a choice of three young adult novels—and incidentally mentioned our final nine-week test, chaos erupted. LaBelle had given me warning, and now everyone in the class was upset.

Didn't I know that *no* teachers taught anything beyond the state assessment test? We were not supposed to do much of anything in class, and there *couldn't* be a nine-weeks test—it was *illegal*. Helen mentioned the date of the test on the syllabus—a syllabus I had been repeatedly told no one remembered, could find, or ever used—and said I needed to change it now. There could be *no* nine-weeks test. *I had better check all this out now.* We went on with class, but I felt well-warned, and I assured the students that I would follow up.

I was fairly incredulous, but the students were so adamant and so loud that I wondered if they could be right. Stranger things have happened: Maybe this was a school where all teaching indeed ceased after the state assessment, and the nine-weeks tests were suspended. I checked the school handbook, I talked with Terry and Kasey, and there was no such memo, no such agreement, and the nine-weeks test was standard, at least on paper. But for the students, *I* was clearly out of bounds, breaking some sort of tacit agreement, violating what at least some teachers at Live Oak must have practiced in the late spring after the state test. The resentment about continuing on with class seemed insurmountable.

Certainly students were aware of the tests' consequences. Students who scored well were recognized in letters delivered to the class and were cited publicly in an all-school assembly. In addition, for those who had passed, end-of-course exams would be suspended. In an effort to get students to care about the tests and the results, it seemed quite possible that the rest of the year's curriculum faded in importance.

Fortunately, the whole incident had a relatively happy end. The choice of young adult novels and the subsequent multiple creative projects were the most successful venture we had had all semester, so there was ultimately no issue with work. But the students' feeling of being betrayed—again, no one seemed to have read the second nine-weeks syllabus where it was clear that the semester would continue beyond the state test—was lingering. It would show up later in the student assessment of the course. And, at least with the students, I lost a whole lot by insisting. As they told me repeatedly when they evaluated the class later, it was clear that I would not listen and would not compromise. For my students, once the state test was taken, all bets were off, all real work should cease, and I was one of the few teachers who wouldn't cooperate.

Again, school culture may have set my student's reaction only too precisely. Martinez and Bray (2002) acknowledge the "unintended consequences of standards-based accountability systems" (p. 39) and although their research concentrated on students who were unable to meet the test requirements, consequences also abound for those, like my students, who cleared the test barrier only too handily. Students at Live Oak High School were told repeatedly how important the tests were and how much the tests mattered not only for the students but for the school and the school district. When test scores came out, they were immediately reported to the students and, if the students did well, they received privileges, recognition, and also were exempted from final (not nine-weeks, but final) exams. Ashton in particular scored very well on the writing segment of the exam—no surprise there—and was given a certificate and later honored at an assembly. All of this recognition and reward for the state high-stakes test was understandable, but when placed in the context of a "regular" class, it made going on to the end of the semester anticlimactic and, as the students told me, just pretty unnecessary. From my students' perspective, I had clearly misread the memo, a communication that told us all that the major purpose of the semester's course was a single one: to prepare for the state test.

8

CONFLICT OF EXPECTATIONS

In the middle of the journey . . .
I came to my senses in a dark forest,
For I had lost the straight path.
—Dante, *The Inferno* (c. 1308/1968, Canto I, 11.1–3)

Most teachers will tell you that certain classes make for a very long school year, especially when there are tensions with students or groups of students. Despite some success and connections with individuals, the class as a whole and I were not an easy mix. Although Ashton and Karol and Mary continued to be good students and good citizens, some of the other members of the class did not seem so inclined. Sharon became hostile when I circulated during small-group work, using frowns and body language to signal that it was time for me to *go away now*. Alex became selectively deaf when asked questions in class; Latosha often responded as if I were speaking in Spanish or French. I persisted every day, but during one large-group discussion I realized that the lack of success with everyone was beginning to grate on me. The conflict of expectations was getting serious.

I LOSE MY TEMPER

Alice, well-regarded by her classmates and an important force with her peers, was not happy in our class. Due to scheduling snafus, she had to take junior English when she was a senior, and she had already been accepted to college. It was the spring of her senior year, and she was ready to move on. There was a real distance between her and other students, and although she loved sharing her journal entries, mostly those that were free choice, she saw herself as older, more mature, and clearly headed for the larger world. Alice was filled with interests in horses, her friends, and the Quaker religion—which she made clear she liked a whole lot but also made clear she did not practice (organized religion was, to Alice, out of the question). At one point, Alice and I had conferred about changing totally the focus of the first essay. She asked about this in class and when we talked one-on-one, Alice had not been pleased when I could not see how taking on the persona of a German exchange student—she had met one at Live Oak last year— could adequately address the topic of images of America in the pieces of literature we had read. I questioned her, and Alice, it seemed, was seriously miffed. So miffed that she did not submit any rough draft, and her final was written about the German exchange student anyway. At any rate, I did not think the essay was successful, and I suggested revision—no, it didn't address the topic, and one of the most obvious weaknesses was that Alice's knowledge of Germany and modern Europe was pretty shaky.

Alice never did revise the piece. No problem, that was her choice, but Alice and I were not close after that.

Thus, when it came time to tackle one of our essays, based on a chapter from Judy Blunt's (2002) *Breaking Clean*, Alice, when questioned, could not, would not give any specifics as to why she so intensely disliked the chapter. It was "boring," it was "dumb" was about all she could muster. The class nodded enthusiastically. I wondered again if anyone had read this amazing description of a western blizzard that decimated the family's cattle ranch and almost killed Blunt's father. So, I persisted, let's move on: What might have motivated Blunt to write this? Alice chose to answer: "She's a whiner," she said, "she's writing to get attention and for the money." She smiled at me after this remark.

The class was silent, either in approval or indifference. I wasn't sure why, but at that moment, for some reason, my frustrations with Trailer 11 coalesced. I was furious. It was amazing to me that anyone could retreat to such simplistic assumptions, and I said so. No, Blunt did not write this just to get attention and make money, what else? But there was no *what else* for Alice, or the class, and when Sharon used the identical mantra later to describe another piece we were reading—"She's whiney. She wrote it to get attention and money"—and then smiled at me, I knew the class had recognized my weak spot and was hoping I just might show anger again. No way—I kept my voice even this time, but also recognized that it was becoming overly important to me that students understand the literature and not retreat behind shallow characterizations. I realized I was losing perspective and, this time at least, possibly losing control. Not good.

THE FIELD TRIP TRAVESTY

In January, at the very beginning of my return to high school teaching, I had asked students about their interest in collaborating with students from another school in the area. A teaching friend's eleventh-grade class would also be reading *The Great Gatsby* (Fitzgerald, 1925/1995), and their culminating activity would be a Socratic Seminar discussion. My students had never experienced such a seminar, and I thought it might be interesting and motivating to arrange for the two sets of students from two different schools to work together. I proposed this and a field trip, where we could meld classes for a period or two, discuss the novel, and then all eat lunch and socialize at the host school. My students had been positive about the idea in January and, accordingly, I had met with the teacher at the other school, we had selected a mutually agreeable date for the classes to meet, and we had planned how the actual class with both sets of students might unfold. Reading schedules were coordinated, materials for the Socratic Seminar were exchanged, permission regulations were discussed, and money was set aside to treat the students to pizza.

When I brought up this excursion idea to the students once again in March, now at the beginning of the second nine weeks, my students were again positive. The only negative aspect was when I once again mentioned the name of the school. There were some frowns; students knew where we were going but perhaps had forgotten. The school was a regional school for gifted students, and students were admitted by application only; some expressed fear of talking with those "smart kids." This, of course, gave me the opening to observe that the smart kids were not as smart as the students assumed (I had actually taught an African literature unit to tenth graders there), nor were my own students without skills themselves, and that I hoped the other students' "giftedness" would not be a barrier. No one continued the discussion. I thought the students seemed reassured.

So on I went. I gathered materials about Socratic Seminar structure and set up some advance assignments regarding questions on *The Great Gatsby* so that we could role-play a bit before we actually met with the other students. I also set up a voluntary student e-mail pairing so that, a few weeks before the field trip, my Live Oak students could write to another student of their choice (lists of names and e-mail addresses were circulated) to get some sort of personal exchange going before we all met face-to-face. Interestingly, some of my students knew some of the students at the other school, and talked about their knowledge. Girls made sure they chose boys, and for some, it was important to examine first names so that racial pairing would be appropriate. Of course, we needed a bus and permission for the field trip. After the administration okayed it, Kasey, Terry, and I arranged for the transportation; worked up an informational permission form; and over our signatures sent it, through the students, to the parents 10 days before the actual trip. The information was also posted on the electronic bulletin board for the class.

The result? Something I would never have anticipated.

The discussion questions I asked students to write for practice were dismal, and even after the presentation of a model and a second assignment option, they remained poorly done. A Socratic Seminar did not seem to be a structure that the students seemed either to understand or to like, and whatever class work I did was not breaking the impasse. I wondered how well this would go once we got to the school, but honestly felt that discussion would be discussion, and that the whole experience would more than likely have unanticipated benefits. So I encouraged the students and told them that we would just adjust and probably do well. As for the e-mail exchange, only one or two students e-mailed their chosen counterparts at the other school. This e-mailing was voluntary, as I had made clear—how could I *require* students to make friendly overtures by e-mail?—but the truly tepid response was surprising to me. Even with free time and a computer lab near, few took the time; connecting with other kids just did not seem important or interesting.

The biggest surprise was to come. The week before the trip, I had received about six signed permission slips from the 22 students in my class. I was concerned and reminded the class that I needed the signed slips *right now*; as everyone knew, we could not go without parental permission. At the end of that week, three more permission slips appeared, and another reminder from me: This trip was in their hands, and without permission, we could not go. I had thought about this the night before and was ready to make a shift. Sure enough, the last class day before the trip, only two more permissions slips came in. Eleven of 22 was not sufficient: I told the students we would not be going. I'd cancel the bus, notify the school, call the teacher at the other school, and we would do something with *The Great Gatsby* other than a Socratic Seminar discussion. I expected an uproar, a protest, an alternative plan, but none came. In fact, the expected expressions of dissatisfaction lasted less than a minute.

But obviously I hadn't done enough. At the end of that particular class, Neal came up to me, shaking his head. There was no reason to cancel. All I needed to do was get on the phone that very night, call all the parents individually, and either get their permission over the phone or remind them to have the slips ready when we boarded the bus the next morning. If somehow that didn't work out and the slips did not appear at 8:00 a.m., we'd just go back to Trailer 11 or, even better, those who had signed would go to the other school, and the remaining students could have a substitute and stay in regular class.

I couldn't help but wince, thinking of the responsibility issue, the time it would take for me to call—and reach—the parents, the making up a new set of plans in case the trip did not go on, the alternative plans for the students left behind, the calling and canceling an hour before our arrival at the other school if the trip did not materialize. I couldn't do it. The phrase *locus of control* kept shrieking in my mind. For Neal, it was clear that *I* was the issue. All *I* needed to do was to make even more effort, and the field trip would be salvaged. But I couldn't do it. For me, it was clear that the parents were not the problem, and somehow the bad atmosphere in Trailer 11 had escalated. I had opened the door; students would not, as is their ultimate right, walk through. Looking at who had not turned in their permission slips, I saw clique patterns and groups of friends, and I wondered if this project had been doomed from the beginning, and I was just not plugged in. For whatever reason, declining or derailing this trip—which was it?—was powerful for some students.

As promised, we did not discuss *The Great Gatsby* in a Socratic Seminar but had a test. As usual, I used the student questions and student-selected quotations and ideas. As usual, one-half of the students did very well, and one-half did not do so well. There were 11 As, 2 Bs, 1 C, 5 Ds, and 3 Fs. At the end of the semester, students were emphatic that *The Great Gatsby* was not their favorite piece of literature. For my part, I didn't care if I ever saw it again.

9

SOME GOOD STUFF
AND SOME OTHER STUFF

If it is dark
when this is given to you,
have care for its content
when the moon shines.
—Robert Creeley, "A Form of Women" (1962/1991, p. 48)

Despite such events as the resistance after the state test and the smashed field trip, there were connections with students and with learning. There was, indeed, good stuff with this class beyond the first blush of enthusiasm and energy and despite the research paper problems with deadlines and parental wrath. For one, I count among the successes the research paper—at least for some students. A greater triumph, though, was one discussion that seemed important and interesting; in addition, there were two projects in which most students were creative, engaged, and successful.

THE DISCUSSION THAT WORKED

Death of a Salesman (Miller, 1949/1998) was, I thought, remarkable in the discussions that students had about the play. The double standard of Willy Loman—both praising his wife Linda as a saint only to turn on her with verbal abuse—was a repeated topic that occurred, and one day, after reading and viewing part of the play with Dustin Hoffman as the main character, it finally happened. The students actually engaged in a topic and appeared to listen to each other. In this gender-biased class, many of the female students wanted to talk about Willy's reaction to Linda, and their comments were passionate and pointed. For my part, as I occasionally did, I sat in the back of the class, but this time it worked. The students no longer focused on me as the teacher and center and arbiter—they turned to each other and for almost 10 minutes discussed Willy's language and Linda's choice to remain meek with him but hard with her sons. The only remarkable aspect, however, is that this kind of engagement never happened again.

THE PROJECTS THAT CLICKED

Two projects that also were successful were the movie trailers for the classic short stories (although it was clear that members of some groups not only had not read the stories but honestly didn't understand them) and the final project with the young adult novels. The students did indeed love the novels, as I predicted, and I received excellent work from some students who, like Susan, had done virtually nothing very successful during the semester.

The Movie Trailers

The school district curriculum mandated a variety of genres, and traditional classic short stories were on the list. Considering the class's focus on Media Literacy, however, it seemed to me that using these stories as a basis for a video would be smart. I have always found movie trailers interesting, and in recent years they have become more and more artful. So making a move trailer seemed a great idea to incorporate the media skills of the students with the prescribed curriculum. So I browsed through anthologies and chose a menu of six stories. In class, I gave students a sketch for each and asked them to indicate their first and second choices. Then I set up groups of four in accordance with the stories the students had chosen.

Using "The Magic Barrel" (Malamud, 1954/1978), "To Build a Fire" (London, 1908/1978), "Chickamauga" (Bierce, 1891/1978), "Chrysanthemums" (Steinbeck, 1937/1978), "A & P" (Updike, 1962/1978), and "A Good Man Is Hard to Find" (O'Connor, 1953/1978), students were invited to create their own one-minute movie trailer (see Appendix B for details). Students also evaluated the videos in an all-class sharing.

Despite some stutters, the student work in the project was very successful. The camera microphones were never strong enough to pick up clear audio, but when we viewed the final products, most were creative and evocative. One was, at least by my assessment, astonishing, in that it captured perfectly some of the real subtlety of the Flannery O'Connor story and showed maturity and artistic flair. As with any group project, though, not all efforts were successes. One student pair did not understand the story on almost any level—despite the work we did on each story in groups—and their video showed it. Yet they were the only one of the six groups to falter.

Once again, school regulations loomed. The group filming "A & P" —a short story about two girls who wandered into a resort grocery store dressed in swimsuits—was filmed using two girls, one of whom wore a halter top and jeans to simulate the bathing suit. Somehow Ms. Wood got wind of this attire and indicated that *no one* in the class could see the video but myself—as it might appeal to prurient interest. The class was not amused, nor was I, but the "A & P" video, accordingly, had to be evaluated only by myself.

The YA Lit Books

Another success was the use of young adult books. I did book talks for all three, and students could choose to work with *Buried Onions* (Soto, 1997), *When the Emperor Was Divine* (Otsuka, 2002), or *Witness* (Hesse, 2001). The fact that this assignment worked well was truly remarkable since it came at the very end of the semester when students were not interested in working further: The state tests had been negotiated, and apathy was high.

Students were able to choose the book they wanted and could choose from a number of projects (see Appendix C for full details).

What made these projects work with this class? There was choice, which although not always the silver bullet I had hoped for, seemed to work at this point in the semester. There was also the element of surprise. Students could do something unusual with traditional literature (e.g., make a video), and students could do something creative with a different genre, young adult literature. And, as I suspected, the three YA novels were appealing and interesting to students. Though all three choices dealt with unfamiliar settings and two depended upon historical events, *Buried Onions, Witness,* and *When the Emperor Was Divine* were relatively solid successes. They were quick and accessible and did not make students struggle with comprehension and vocabulary as had some of the earlier readings. By contrast, the nonfiction essays, *The Great Gatsby,* and even the classic American short stories proved, on reading, difficult and at times uninteresting to students.

WHEN BEST PRACTICE MEETS SCHOOL CULTURE

So there was some good stuff. In particular, the beginning of every class went well as students did write in their journals, did share their comments, and I got a chance to write with them and also share. Some of the journal responses were really well done, witty, wise, and crafted, and students did seem to enjoy not only the required entries, but the fact that almost every day there was choice to write on something not mandated. When we also shared these aloud in class, most students seemed to appreciate what they heard. There were nods, chuckles, and appreciative smiles.

But the transaction seemed to stop there. Other than Neal—who had loved my comments and questions on his writing and had communicated back—most of the students made no response when I collected their journals four times during the semester and read and wrote back to them. I made observations, shared personal responses, and asked questions, but no one took the bait.

Best practice, even shaped to this class and this group of students, seemed less than riveting to this group than I had anticipated: The choices they had were just more school choices. Yes, they could choose one of six short stories on which to base their movie trailers and, yes, they could choose one of three young adult novels and, yes, they had choices within choices for the research paper. But as noted before, at no time did the factor of choice seem that motivational or inspirational. In addition, the fact that student questions and choices on tests determined the test itself seemed not worthy of much notice. In particular, the power of students to select the vocabulary words, determine how they would be tested, and use the consistent pretesting of that vocabulary to prepare was not, to my observation, seen as helpful at all. The revision groups were not effective beyond the first 10 minutes of consultation, and open opportunities to revise papers that were not initially successful were rarely taken. I circulated constantly during group work—stopping, listening, answering questions if needed—but it often appeared to me that my presence was not necessary.

Although I had to juggle mandated curricular requirements, I also wanted the class to have some relation to the real world. At the beginning of the semester, as the United States was gearing up to begin the Iraq War, in discussions students had articulated anger at the government, the daily school-mandated recitation of the Pledge of Allegiance, and the inequities of American society. The coming Iraq War seemed to disturb them a great deal, and I allowed the conversation on the topic to flow. The war discussion moved into issues of immigration, the plight of the American Indian, and the definition of *patriotism*. But when the war actually began, and I brought in material and urged students to do the same, it fell flat. I mentioned news reports from CNN and other sources, and there were blank faces. Giving extra credit for new and old "war words" and phrases that were coming fast and furious (*embed*, *surgical strike*, *shock and awe*, *freedom fries*) or bringing into class a recent news report on what was happening to schools in Iraq was greeted with indifference. I dangled the bait, and no one bit. Once the war was on, the class was not engaged in the topic at all.

While I did make Neal feel that he was a writer, and my intervention did seem to spur Susan to some sort of energy at the end of the semester, I never was able to break through to Alex or Latosha, neither of whom did much during the year to make significant academic progress. In both instances, with both students, calls home to the parents were not satisfactory; Alex's mother had heard the complaints before and felt it was the teacher's and school's responsibility to spur him toward academic performance. Latosha's mother was unimpressed by my dire assessment of her daughter's capabilities, and when she shared the conversation with Latosha, there was resentment and lingering suspicion. Alice and Ellen Patton left the semester with a sense of injury resulting from my questions regarding their work and my judgment of their efforts.

The breakthrough of Jackie and Helen in their research papers, Anthony's continuing excellence in vocabulary, and the fine essay writing of Ashton and Karol and Mary were satisfactions. But I believe much of this achievement was not directly due to my teaching; some students came to class with these skills developed and, in our semester together, only continued to refine them. Lee, who had taken a liking to me from the very first, continued to show her appreciation and kindness, and left a note on my desk that thanked me for teaching ("you are one of the most caring teachers I've met and that means alot to me") and asked me to come visit her in school next year. Starr, elusive as ever, left with shy smiles.

It was, in many ways, just like teaching can occasionally be, with hits and misses, but when a sense of satisfaction and engagement is elusive, the learning almost seems overshadowed. As Linda McNeil (1986, 2000) maintains, to merit student engagement, we must provide high-quality content and instruction. I attempted to give these to the students in my class, but student engagement, at least at the level that I wished, was hard fought and rarely won in Trailer 11 at Live Oak High School.

What I saw in my return to high school was, once again, the power of the culture and of student themselves to limit and determine what and how much was learned. Successful classes demand mutual student and teacher engagement and activity; if students are passive or unwilling, if what is offered is not engaging or seems to call for more effort than students bargain for, activities that some teachers initiate—or even cherish—will not be effective. For my part, no amount of cheerleading, prior student assent (which I had somewhat misjudged), or persistence could break certain patterns. There were successes in some projects and in some classroom activities, but never to the extent that, even at my most pessimistic, I had anticipated. When students decided that the answer was *no*, my *yes* was ineffective.

When I calculated final grades for the second nine weeks, 14 of the 22 students received As or Bs. Yet seven of the 22 students had not turned in significant work, and their grades were affected. Two failed for the nine weeks; two earned Ds, and four received Cs.

When I concluded my work in Trailer 11, the students did a little presentation in class and gave me a card and a paperweight; there was a round of applause. I thanked them, and they all smiled at me. Terry later swore she had not suggested or arranged this last gesture. It was unexpected and touching, and with that I left Live Oak High School and Trailer 11.

But I didn't stop thinking about the experience; it was ultimately puzzling to me, and what I had anticipated happening during the spring semester had not occurred. How could I make sense of the five months in Trailer 11 and my retracing of the journey? At the end, what did the students really feel? And how did this experience match that of other teachers? I looked for some answers.

10

Assessment: The Students and Other Teachers

Tacit bargaining [between teachers and students] usually takes the form of offering a more predictable and rote curriculum or a curriculum with fewer serious intellectual challenges in exchange for more docile and pliant student body. . . . Thus student pressures to reduce complexity and reduce intellectual burdens are an important part of the circumstances in which teachers must teach.

—Mary M. Kennedy, *Inside Teaching* (2005, pp. 16–17)

Looking backward at the view from Trailer 11, what did it mean? I looked to a number of sources for answers and, of course, I started with the students.

WHAT THE STUDENTS HAD TO SAY

I did not ask my students to assess their semester experience immediately at the conclusion of the class in mid-June. At the time, I was not sure that my students, who I felt were still miffed about having to do work in the weeks following the state assessment test, would be able to surmount their disappointment and objectively assess the class as a whole. So I waited for summer to come and go and devised a brief, anonymous questionnaire (see Appendix D) for the subsequent fall. The students' new teacher was more than willing to administer the questionnaire in his class. So in early September, 18 of the original 22 students, still together as a cohort, voluntarily answered about four dozen questions about the course content and activities using a five-degree Likert scale: strongly agree, agree, no opinion, disagree, strongly disagree. There were also five constructed-response questions and one final, open-ended question at the end of the questionnaire, which asked for any other comments.

The results of the questionnaire showed a healthy mix of responses. Although not every student answered every question (three students declined to answer any of the five constructed-response questions in Section One, and 14 did not answer the open-ended question at the very end of the questionnaire), it appears that the students took the distinctions in the questions (understood/enjoy/learn) fairly seriously. Responses to the questions about the literature section and class activities in Section Two showed that students did not rate all three in the same manner on a consistent basis. Thus, students would cite that they enjoyed an activity and understood it, but did not learn from it or, conversely, did not enjoy an activity but did learn from it.

The number of students who cited "no opinion" on the questions was steady; about four to five students regularly chose that category for a response. Finally, on only one or two questionnaires did students circle the same answer for every question.

SECTION TWO: COURSE CONTENT AND ACTIVITIES

I should not have been surprised, but I admit, I was: The questionnaire indicated that many students did not actually read what was assigned. I did not realize that this nonreading was so widespread, and that fact certainly illuminated some of the difficulties that students experienced and reported in large-group discussion. Also, my perception that students liked reading and working with *Death of a Salesman*—after all, that one large-group discussion was, in my estimation, a class benchmark—was not confirmed by the questionnaire. Similarly, my perception that *The Great Gatsby* was disliked by most students was also not confirmed; students actually did not report hating *Gatsby* that much at all. Also, I felt that the research paper had been really difficult for this class, and expected the ratings to be relatively low in all three categories; they were not.

What was clear, however, is that students' dissatisfaction with continuing the class beyond the state assessment test was strong and pervasive. My late-semester rejection of the students' request to discontinue teaching beyond the testing did show up on the questionnaire: Some students wrote that I was close-minded and not willing to listen to student opinion.

Class Activities

Some of my assumptions were confirmed. My initial belief that students had particularly enjoyed two activities—the creation of a movie trailer based on a short story and the young adult novels and the choice of creative response—was supported by the questionnaire.

The activities that received the highest satisfaction were first, the movie trailer and, tied for second, the journal writing, the small-group work, and the large-group discussions. The creative response activities for the young adult novels were also well-received in all three categories.

What students did not like, enjoy, or learn from was the writing of essays and, despite the student control over the choice of words, the vocabulary study. Both of these activities received very negative ratings in the enjoyment and learning categories; almost half the student respondents ranked these two negatively.

And, as noted before, only a handful of students professed not to enjoy or learn from the research paper. Almost all respondents understood the activity; most enjoyed it and learned from it. Only two respondents even indicated "no opinion" in any of the categories regarding the research paper.

Literature Selections

The opening packet of materials that I had given students at the beginning of the semester containing poetry, song lyrics, and prose excerpts received generally positive responses: Students indicated that the literature in the packet was understood and that they learned from it. About one-third of the students, however, did not particularly enjoy the selections. Similarly, students indicated that the essays we read, despite what

I perceived as difficulties in discussion, were understood and that they learned from them—but that they did not enjoy reading them.

What students really criticized, however, was *Death of a Salesman*, a play that I believed students had understood and enjoyed and which, in my opinion, had generated the best exchange we had ever had. The questionnaire, however, did not confirm all of this: While students indicated that they understood the play, less than one-third enjoyed reading it, and the overwhelming majority indicated that they did not learn from the play. In addition, despite the comments in the open-ended section about deleting *The Great Gatsby* and my strong perception that students detested this novel, the questionnaire indicated differently. The majority of students gave it positive ratings: The students who responded generally understood, enjoyed, and learned from the novel, and a very small number gave it negative ratings. Go figure.

The short stories were well-received in all three categories, but the highest approval rating (again, in all three categories) was reserved for the three young adult novels, from among which students could choose.

SECTION ONE: STUDENTS' OPEN-ENDED ANSWERS

What They Liked/What They Would Change

In general, when asked what they *liked* about our semester course, students cited the group work, the class discussions, the movie trailer assignment, the daily journal writing, and even (from two students) the research paper. Some left the question blank, though, and one wrote, "Nothing."

What students would *change* about the course involved the specifics of the essay questions; the focus of the essays on the course theme did not strike some students as useful. One student suggested choice for all books and the deletion of *The Great Gatsby*.

Advice to Other Students

The answers in this section involved doing the work, paying attention, addressing topics on assignment sheets, and writing a lot. Three students suggested that, as one put it, you should "actually read the stories" and the novels. "Be open 2 change" was one bit of advice, but the same student who wrote that he/she liked "Nothing" in the course also advised students, "Drop it, change teachers."

Personal Advice

Asked what I as a teacher seemed to *understand* and, conversely, what I *needed to know*, students wrote that I needed to be "more open" to their comments and suggestions. This criticism surfaced in no less than five questionnaires and was described as "showing respect" for student opinion. From my perspective, this comment indicates that I was not amenable to making changes, especially regarding work at the end of the semester. For some students, I deduce, that was evidence enough that I did not respect them. Some students also suggested that I give them more time to adjust to the workload (which one of them termed a *college-style class*). One student did not feel I fully appreciated "the unique teenager," and one wrote: "She would not listen to us." Other students felt I understood about the time needed to write and express themselves and knew how to lead a discussion of literature; one called me an "awesome" teacher, and two noted that the course was a good one, and that I was one of the best English teachers he or she had had "my entire school career."

THE LAST QUESTION

General, open-ended comments at the end of the questionnaire were offered only by four students; all of them wrote positive comments about their improvement in writing, and one student even wrote, "I'll miss you this year." Another student offered, "Your teaching is very detailed. That is a good thing." I am not sure what *detailed* teaching means, but I'll take it as a compliment.

In some ways, the students' responses in the questionnaire were not out of line with my assessment of the semester at Live Oak. What I thought students really enjoyed in the course was somewhat confirmed in their answers, and it was good to know that they did respond positively to the journal writing and some of the creative activities. My feeling that students felt angry—even betrayed—regarding my decision to go on teaching beyond the state test was confirmed in many of their answers and was a thread in most of the completed questionnaires. Student comments on the essay writing and the vocabulary were striking in that I would never have assumed that those two aspects of the semester would be so negatively memorable.

Yet no student mentioned the aborted field trip and the other ways that invitations were extended and not accepted. No one opened the possibility that, as Gregory Michie (2005) notes, often for "young people struggling against feelings of powerlessness . . . resistance can be a palpable sign of life" (p. 190). It was not an articulated issue. But what of the range of the course, the control students had over almost all aspects of the testing, and the consistent use of choice? What of the multiple avenues of communication and the rapid and consistent responses to student inquiries and writing? None of these surfaced in any of the students' answers or observations, and I can only conclude that it was either not apparent to them or, more likely, not important.

Reviewing the results of the student questionnaire, I firmly believe that many of the students honestly never connected to what *I* thought was going on in class, how the material and the activities and their own control over what and how and when we did things could be important and engaging. I am relatively sure that most of the 22 students did not share my vision of the class or their own learning, and in some important ways, did not consent to the curriculum or the content.

In this situation, neither content nor methodology appears to be a trump card. As I have written in other contexts, how we organize the teaching and select the subject matter cannot always triumph—and certainly did not in this experience. Whatever bargain I thought I was making with the students and whatever control I thought they were given—over what we did, how, and when—they resisted and at times tried to negotiate a change in rules, and I would not always cooperate. I think that some of them walked away from the experience feeling I did not listen; I walked away knowing that I could not, after some point, compromise.

LOOKING AT THE EXPERIENCE
OF OTHER TEACHERS

This was of course my own experience returning to the high school classroom; there are numerous contemporary accounts of other teachers who have made similar ventures. It had not struck me, until I began returning to these accounts and finding new ones, that very few of them are positive.

One is a piece I published when I served as editor of *English Journal*. In it, Sally Hudson-Ross and Patti McWhorter (1995) wrote of Hudson-Ross's year-long stint in an Atlanta high school. Like myself, Hudson-Ross's interest in returning to the high school classroom was not mild but strong and visceral. She wrote that she wanted to "'go back,' to prove that I could still teach" (p. 46). After observation and preparation, Hudson-Ross taught a full load of five classes for an entire year, exchanging positions with her longtime teaching friend, Patti McWhorter. Hudson-Ross wrote of "overwork and the need for control," and I could empathize:

> I worked harder and harder in order to gain control. I had to help them [the students] see this mattered, that it struck me deeply. I was furious (to myself) with kids who chose to sleep, read slowly, or even just be polite and let me carry on. My classroom became more and more mine, more and more teacher-centered. I was so buried in MY love of writing, MY books, MY curricular vision, that I lost all perspective. . . . I was very hurt that they didn't care. (p. 50)

In particular, especially regarding her effort to get students to read extensively, Hudson-Ross wrote that

> seeing my dreams crushed little by little exhausted me to the point of defeat . . . we can model, we can build rules together for community success, we can strive to bring everyone to books and writing and choice, but [some students] will sneer, read a "baby" book and inform everyone, "you said I could read anything, HA!" Gotcha. (p. 51)

For Hudson-Ross, "the realities of teaching today are far harsher than they were a decade or more ago" (p. 51). I am not sure I could agree that they were *harsher*—my students at Live Oak were rarely openly confrontational and resistant—but they certainly were more skillfully, effectively evasive than the students I taught in years before. Yet I share with Hudson-Ross other points in common: In particular, her feeling of frustration when invitations to learn and engage are declined is familiar territory.

In "Scriptless in High School: Teaching Dreams of a College Professor," Don Daiker (2002) described how for a semester he taught in Princeton High School. Like myself, Daiker prepared carefully for the upcoming experience through classroom observations, conferences with high school teachers, and professional reading. Having never experienced high school teaching, Daiker felt he needed some time with the real thing: "it was guilt that drove me to high school teaching" (p. 3). His assessment, though, was not comforting:

> My four months at Princeton High School constituted the most challenging and difficult teaching assignment I have ever undertaken. Despite thirty years of experience in teaching writing, literature, and education courses at Miami [Ohio] University, I always felt inadequate and unprepared in my high school classrooms. There were some small victories, but many more defeats. (p. 4)

For Daiker, the experience was emotional, and in his account he used a series of nightmare dreams to illustrate his feeling of being utterly "scriptless" in his teaching, repeatedly experiencing "dreams of inadequacy and failure" (p. 7). He noted a real difference between high school and college teaching:

> Teaching high school requires not only more effort but also a more comprehensive self-offering, a fuller giving of the self, a tapping of more and different kinds of energies. High school teachers have to be wiser than college teachers. High school teaching demands more of a total response, requires that you use not only your brains (which is usually enough for college teachers) but your heart and emotions and common sense and good psychology as well. (p. 10)

I could empathize. I did not feel *scriptless*, but I knew well the differing demands of university and high school teaching. The importance of emotional connection—the need for a total response to students and some kind of reciprocity from them—was also clear to me, and when it did not occur regularly in my class, it was more than troublesome. I wanted to be strongly connected to all my students and, in fact, I was not.

Thompson and Louth's (2003) "Radical Sabbaticals: Putting Yourself in Danger" detailed two different sabbatical esperiences. Of interest is Thompson's story of his semester teaching high school. A composition professor curious about how writing was handled in secondary school English classes, Thompson, unlike myself, had never taught at the high school level. Early on, there was concern at his home institution that he had "taken leave of my senses" (p. 149), but he persevered. In a trailer—which he described accurately and acerbically —Thompson made adjustments with his students. His experience reflected much of what I felt in Trailer 11. Regarding one creative assignment, he wrote:

> I had thought this would be a fun assignment—a chance to be creative and maybe to engage in a little drama in the classroom—but the students don't seem to care. The apathy—and from honors students, too—continues to astound me. (p. 155)

Thompson concluded with an assessment of why high school teaching can be so enervating. It may strike veteran high school teachers as naive, but for Thompson it was real:

> I frequently came home from high school beat down rather than revved up. Living with the pressure (self-imposed, I confess, but nevertheless real) of constantly having several stacks of papers to return sapped some of my energy but having to deal every day with the layers of administrative trivia can, like the steady drip-drip-drip of an insignificant stream, slowly undermine anybody's enthusiasm. Keep accurate records of who's in class, who's not, and who's late. Sign grade forms or behavior forms for every student whose parent requests one. Turn in grades every four and a half weeks so parents will know exactly how their children are doing. Meet with everybody who wants a moment of your time. Turn in roll sheets every afternoon. Sign every student's "admit" slip and record whether the absence was excused or unexcused, lawful or unlawful. Turn in extra copies of assignments for students who miss too many days of class. Adjust

your classes today for the pep rally—no, wait, the pep rally has been can-
celled. Give up your classroom so we can do some more testing. I don't
mean to sound negative—I love teaching—but I'm still reeling from the
mental pounding I took daily for four months. (p. 159)

Others in university settings who have returned to the classroom
also note that part of the issue of going back to classroom teaching is
accepting limitations and accepting that victories must be indeed partial. Possibly much of my distress at Live Oak High School involved
my unwillingness *not* to have major success on a daily basis, *not* to
accept that teaching is often routine, difficult, and undramatic. Two
other accounts of returning to the classroom underscore this.

Anne Fairbrother (2003) is a veteran high school teacher who returned to the classroom in order to find a connection between "the ivory
tower and the trenches, the educational front lines" (p. 27). Her return
was not a smooth one:

After five years in graduate school and with a dissertation in progress, I
returned to the high school English classroom, eager to do well by my
students and armed with a language to describe what should happen
there. But for the first six months I was in deep distress. For all the grand
ideas, what I was doing wasn't working. For some students, yes, and
sometimes for many. But often for most, no.

It wasn't just the disconnect between theory and practice, nor was it
simply the dichotomy between what I knew about best practices and the
quotidian reality of the classroom. I knew this wasn't how it should be,
or could be. That I was unprepared for the rudeness and resistance of students in my classes wasn't the whole story, either: I knew why they resisted schooling, but I didn't want them to do it in *my* classroom. And it
wasn't just that, in my first few weeks back, I knew viscerally that schooling in this factory atmosphere that produced drilled and disengaged
young people was no way to educate students. It wasn't even the suffo-
cating and pervasive ethos that students have learned so well and deeply
through the years: that education is irrelevant except for the good grades
that get you the good job.

It wasn't any one of these things. It was all of them, lurking menac-
ingly behind my daily lesson plans, screaming behind my failure, fuel-
ing my anger and frustration, disorienting me into confusion, wounding
me terribly. (p. 27)

Fairbrother's solution was to accept that she was doing the best she could in the situation and to make peace with her sense of inadequacy: "I hadn't failed. I was doing the best I could" (p. 27). More interestingly, however, she concluded: "I found myself in a space that hasn't been adequately scrutinized: the space between how the classroom really is and how it could be—the heart of the matter" (p. 27). Indeed.

In my years teaching at the university level, working with graduate students studying to be high school English teachers, my focus has been on a classroom that is structured and run competently and in which students respond and learn. Certainly my students and I, in discussion, in activities, role-play, field observations, and formal papers, spend time examining what can go awry in instruction and why. We look at what kinds of adjustments teachers can make during a single period or in a unit or semester. We consider the multiple variables that affect instruction, and we try to focus on the shifting relationships between student learning and student behavior. But, like Fairbrother, my necessary focus has been how to structure and run a very good class or set of classes. The space between those "good" classes and the others —which for many reasons and in many ways are not "good"—the disparity between how it is and how it could be, has not, as Fairbrother astutely observes, been scrutinized as fully as needed.

Although his focus is at a different instructional level, the experience of Curt Dudley-Marling (1997) is also pertinent. Dudley-Marling left the university to teach third grade, and in *Living with Uncertainty*, he explored his experience much in the light of J. P. McDonald's (1992) "messy realities of classroom practice." Dudley-Marling noted that "despite all the preparation I'd done and the support I'd received, teaching third grade was difficult" (p. xi). He concluded:

> Teachers must always strive to do their best, but unless teachers are able to work in a context that acknowledges the uncertainties, the ambiguities, the contradictions, and the variability of the human enterprise that teaching is, teaching will continue to be a very stressful occupation with limited opportunities for job satisfaction. The challenge for teachers and teacher educators is to find ways to confront idealized models of the good teacher who succeeds with every student—in which case we blame either the teacher or we blame the student and, if we blame the student he or

she must bear the stigma of educational labels. . . . The current situation is a set-up that makes it difficult for large numbers of teachers and students to feel good about themselves and their work. (p. 188)

Certainly, Dudley-Marling's conclusion is very near how I assessed my time in Trailer 11. "Limited opportunities for job satisfaction" ring very true—and if it is hard for "teachers and their students to feel good about themselves and their work," the teaching hours can be long indeed. Some of my hours at Live Oak High School seemed to stretch out, and it became an effort on some days to stay positive and to stay focused.

Finally, my colleague Deborah Appleman, writing with Susan Hynds (1997), discussed her return to teach high school literature in an urban classroom and the limitations of response-centered teaching. Along with other insights, Appleman observed that "no preparation in any of my professional domains could have prepared me to deal adequately" (p. 273) with any number of classroom issues. Going back, Appleman notes, "walking our talk" is often harder than might first be imagined. In my case, walking the talk was absolutely my focus, but its results were often unanticipated.

Every one of these accounts, different as they may be, reflects parts of my semester at Live Oak High School. While the struggle stories of well-meaning university professors who have never taught in the high school classroom might be easily explained and even dismissed, what of the others? Veteran teachers with classroom experience—committed, focused, and prepared—also report varying degrees of failure and inadequacy. They also seem to have left the experience of returning to the secondary (and in the case of Dudley-Marling, the elementary) classroom with new respect for the difficulties of teaching well, teaching every day, and teaching effectively. These relatively melancholy accounts are consistent with what I found in Trailer 11, and paying attention to them is, for me, important. As Michie (2005) observes in *See You When We Get There: Teaching for Change in Urban Schools*, "bringing the voices of teachers center stage is not just a methlolodological issue—it's a political one as well" (p. 184). If schools are to change, what teachers know as classroom reality is central to the discussion. And, in addition, what teachers know needs to be more prominent in discussion in teacher preparation texts, classes, and programs. As Marilyn

Cochran-Smith (2006) notes, "A small but promising trend in teacher education is the effort by some teacher educators to work simultaneously within and against the larger education system" (p. 22). Although we do not want to discourage those who wish to enter the classroom, the daily realities and limitations of real teaching in real settings may not be capturing the attention they deserve, both in the professional literature and in university programs.

WHAT THEIR CURRENT TEACHER HAD TO SAY

About two-thirds through the fall semester after my teaching at Live Oak High School, I contacted the current teacher of my 22 students and asked if he would be willing to meet with me. An eight-year veteran who had been at Live Oak for three of those eight, Robert Dalton had distributed the questionnaire and was willing to make some time to talk. We met at a local coffee shop, and we talked for a few hours about our mutual students, their work, their performance, his assignments, and his adjustments in class.

Dalton, a white man in his early thirties, was calm and deliberate as he noted that the students were not what he had expected. The term *honors* kept recurring in his conversation, and Dalton said he could not see that distinction as applicable to the group. Issues of maturity, work ethic, and understanding of what would be waiting for them the next year in college were all cited by Dalton. For him there were some bright exceptions, but generally he did not rate the class as performing well.

For Dalton, the key to the group was that they had been together as a class since ninth grade and seemed to dislike each other. He had tried large-group discussions during the first month of the fall semester but when, like I did, he saw the resulting bickering and criticism, he ceased the practice entirely. Now for each class he began using a traditional and set format: He gave notes, handed out worksheets and assignments, held a short review and discussion, and tested the students. The students, he thought, seemed happier in that instructional mode and appeared to want to know what was *required*. Like myself, Dalton found that the group did not seem to listen when any one person spoke. Unlike myself, he had an issue in the beginning with students coming to class on time. Now that the adjustments had been made, though, Dalton admitted that he was almost enjoying teaching these students.

What did Dalton wish he knew before he started teaching this class? Three things: "how much they like to fight each other"; "that they like taking notes; I talk/ you write, this they can do"; that they will not do independent work. Dalton noted that the group is "kind of like a *note* class—they take notes."

Parents for this teacher had not been problematic. Yet, Dalton wondered how "spoiled" the students were and cited a meeting between an assistant principal and Sharon, noting with some awe that Sharon also confronted the principal Ms. Wood and had literally shouted at her during the conference.

Dalton did not communicate to the students the course schedule or requirements on a regular basis. He did not provide notes on the white board or a syllabus on paper copies, and he did not use the Live Oak electronic bulletin board. There was no choice in the reading or assignments; the literature used was canonical (*Beowulf, Macbeth,* Mary Shelley's *Frankenstein*); and there were no activities that built on media literacy skills in film and video.

Did the students ever talk about last spring semester, even to kevetch about their teacher? Never, he said, other than the fact that they all agreed they hated *The Great Gatsby* (a comment that seems odd considering the questionnaire results—why didn't they cite *Death of a Salesman*?).

The experience of Dalton was of real interest to me, and what I have tentatively concluded is that he, like some long-term teachers and survivors in the classroom, has more than one mode of teaching. When, as Dalton assessed the group early on, he found little success with creative and inquiry approaches, he switched gears without remorse. The result was a template of giving notes, requiring worksheets, and testing, all of which seemed to satisfy both the students and the curricular requirements.

After talking with Dalton, it seemed clearer to me that I entered Trailer 11 at Live Oak High School with one mode of teaching and could not—would not—alter it. Further, my bedrock allegiances to that teaching meant that I could not quickly or fully capture the Live Oak student work ethic and sense of responsibility. For me, the consequence of shifting instruction to a more traditional pattern—giving notes, testing notes—would have been a loss, as students would not have had the opportunity to be engaged in the way I wanted and valued and in which I was wholeheartedly invested. On the other hand, Dalton felt that he knew well where he could put his energies and where they were not useful. His adjustment and sense of reality were more than immediate survival skills; possibly, they ensured that he would stay teaching for many years to come and certainly meant that he would not be as agonized as I had found myself.

From my students themselves, from the accounts of other teachers, and from teacher Robert Dalton emerged some lessons, lessons learned and relearned.

II

Lessons Learned and Relearned

The habits of schooling are deep, powerful, and hard to budge.
—Deborah Meier, *The Power of Their Ideas* (1995, p. 141)

During my semester in Trailer 11, for an admittedly limited time, I was able to revisit some verities and to relive some relatively unchanging aspects of teaching in a comprehensive high school. Also, I had the chance to compare some differences between teaching when I first began my career and teaching today. I came to the conclusion that there remain real constraints and limits as to what any individual teacher can accomplish in a school, and that many of the constraining factors are the reality of secondary education in today's America.

TREATIES IN THE CLASSROOM

One reality is the place of *treaties* in the comprehensive high school. As the authors of *The Shopping Mall High School* (Powell, Farrar, & Cohen, 1985) maintained years ago:

> Treaties are about the extent to which classroom participants want to re-alize that potential [to engage the mind and develop the capacity to think]. Many [students] do, but most do not. (p. 117)

Twenty years ago, *The Shopping Mall High School* served up an in-dictment of the American high school's structure and content. Look-ing to the future, the authors did not see the comprehensive high school changing much at all, and wrote that the American high school "is likely to withstand efforts to dismantle it" because "too many teenagers are served in the way they want to be served, and too many school professionals willingly provide the services" (p. 309). *Shopping Mall* explored treaties: tacit bargains made between teachers and students in which both agree, essentially, not to ask too much of each other. Teachers specifically would not require onerous tasks of students—and students, in turn, would cooperate and be pleasant:

> Conflict is rarely the way classroom participants come to terms with one another. . . . Agreement is far more common than antagonism. . . . Teachers and students have more subtle ways of accommodating either differences or similarities: they arrange deals or treaties that promote mutual goals or that keep the peace. (pp. 67–68)

This sounds benign and possibly even positive; who could work well in a classroom where conflict continually prevails? But the power of the treaty, as the authors of *Shopping Mall* contended, was far more insidious:

> Despite curricular variety and choice, many students have no incentives to learn what is offered but wish to graduate nevertheless. . . . It is one kind of problem to strive for institutional esprit when students and teachers are equally committed to engaging with many different subjects. It is quite another to forge a community of learners when the issue at stake is whether learning itself is valued. (p. 117)

Linda M. McNeil (1986), in *Contradictions of Control*, made much these same observations and also pushed the argument further. She found that the frequent result of treaties was a mind-numbing boredom and lack of intellectual engagement in classrooms. For McNeil, the teaching and learning enterprise had become seriously poisoned at the source, affecting what teachers actually present to students in the form of content. McNeil argued that teachers, in an effort to maintain a semblance of power or control in school, actually diminished what they taught—their content—and created "brief, 'right' answers, easily transmitted, easily answered, easily graded [in order to accommodate] to a school where their only power came from the classroom" (p. 157). McNeil observed:

> Adults who visit high-school classrooms are often struck by the dullness of the lessons. Those who visit systematically note the overwhelming prevalence of boring content, dull presentations and bored but patient students. . . . The dull presentations are not caused merely by poor teacher preparation or teacher burnout, but by deliberate, often articulated, decisions teachers have made to control the students by controlling the content. . . . Defensive, controlling teaching does more than make content boring; it transforms the subject content from "real world" knowledge into "school knowledge," an artificial set of facts and generalizations whose credibility lies no longer in its authenticity as a cultural selection but in its instrumental value in meeting the obligations teachers and students have within the institution of schooling. . . .
>
> As the course content is transformed into "school knowledge," there is little incentive for the student to become involved in that content. It is there to be mastered, traded for a grade and, as some students have said, deliberately forgotten afterward. (p. 191)

Some 15 years later, in *Contradictions of School Reform: Educational Costs of Standardized Testing*, McNeil (2000) returned to this topic and recalled the "defensive teaching" she first investigated:

> The teachers recognized full well that if the school were smooth-running and few students failed their courses, then the administration would be pleased, and that any extra efforts—to develop an interesting curriculum, to assign and grade student research papers, to stay late to meet with students wanting extra help—would not only not be rewarded but also be disdained as unnecessary. The students knew that if they exerted at least minimum effort, then they would pass their required courses. (p. 15)

This picture haunts me. It is compelling and, more to the point, pertinent so many years after it was first written and then revisited by McNeil. In Trailer 11, the teacher efforts regarding curriculum, innovative activities, and response to student work were not viewed by most of the 22 students as important—or as important as I thought they should be. Students who did not come to class when assignments were due did not appear unduly concerned. Indeed, when much of the point of a school year is to pass a single high-stakes test—a reality that is present not only in the semester I spent at Live Oak High School but also across the country—the result is a narrowing of the curriculum and a diminishing of the students' level of intellectual engagement.

My own graduate students, preparing to teach high school and middle school, log approximately 50 hours in two different classrooms located in two of four local school districts before entering their own full-time, semester-long student teaching. During their observations in the journals they keep and in our subsequent discussions, they often report McNeil's sense of dullness and boredom. Recently, I have come to wonder if what my students describe may be more than the ennui generated by watching, not doing; my students write in their journals regarding some sections of classes where from their perspective literally nothing happens, where teachers ask questions and teachers answer those questions, where worksheets reign. Is this confirming evidence of what McNeil describes? Certainly once teachers make it clear that students are to fit themselves into narrow boxes, they can rarely expect that students will exercise much of the intellectual life: questioning, challenging, exploring. I have always maintained that when teachers convey to students that they do have minds and lives of their own, desires, ideals—that they are not so different from their teachers—then vibrant classroom situations are often the result. At least that is the theory. Yet, for many of my university students, observing in the schools, such vibrancy is often notably absent—as it was in Trailer 11, where one teacher's belief in student intellectual efficacy was not persuasive.

Neither *Contradictions of Control* nor *The Shopping Mall High School* is current. My own graduate students' experiences and observation journals, while current, do not comprise rigorous research. Yet all capture what may be one of the most intractable problems in many high school classrooms: Treaties are still enacted on a daily basis. This is not always negative; when its enactment helps to resolve small issues of values, an unspoken treaty can be a positive influence. When, on the other hand, such a treaty becomes, wholesale, an instrument to blunt the intellectual exchange of the classroom, its enactment dooms students and schools to mediocrity. For any teacher, it is not possible to present complex, nuanced content continually; when, however, content is always reduced to simplistic answers and response, it is not worth students'—or teachers'—time.

Observing other classes at Live Oak before I taught there in spring, I watched Terry, a second-year teacher, with her ninth-grade students who were reading *To Kill a Mockingbird* (Lee, 1960/1999). The novel was one of Terry's favorites, and she brought to the classroom huge enthusiasm and energy, if not a great deal of experience. Sitting in the back of her class for a series of weeks, it seemed to me that the students did little more than tolerate Terry's love for *Mockingbird* and for Atticus and Jem and Scout and Tom Robinson; to all appearances, students were not similarly engaged. This became apparent when, class after class, Terry used virtually the same approach to initiate discussion of the chapters that students had read in class.

While I observed, the scenario never varied. After the reading of each chapter, Terry would place on the overhead projector a sheet with 10 to 15 handwritten questions. And apparently, students knew the drill. Terry would read the handwritten question aloud, using all her enthusiasm and positive manner, pause ever so briefly, and then would almost immediately plunge on with the answer. Her wait time between question and answer was a few seconds at most; question after question, Terry either supplied the answer herself, or, at best, would receive a one-word or one-phrase answer from students. From the students there was no sustained discussion, no exploration, no citation of detail, even for a book that Terry obviously loved and which the students were clearly reading in class.

When I talked to Terry about this procedure—which she consistently repeated with every chapter of the novel and with the same predictable result—she replied that while she knew it was not particularly effective, it seemed to achieve what she wanted. Her goals were recall of the novel's details, and, further, the students behaved well while she did the exercise and, most likely, were "getting" the answers. From my perspective, Terry's students were mostly uninvolved. They knew that if they simply continued what they were used to doing, Terry would eventually answer all the queries or, at most, only a few members of the class would need to engage. With the best of intentions but the deadliest of results, the treaty was signed, sealed, and delivered.

TREATIES AND INSTRUCTIONAL IDEALS

Like its sisters across the country, Live Oak High School, a contemporary American comprehensive high school, is a vision of breadth and depth. What it purports to accomplish, the skills and attitudes it wishes to inculcate, are ambitious and wide-reaching, even global. The mission statement of Live Oak High School articulates its high ideals:

> The vision . . . is to provide a safe and quality educational environment, which cultivates self-accountability and life-long learning through instruction, as well as develop citizenship through community and global awareness. Problem solving, critical thinking and technological skills will be incorporated within all areas of curricula. The faculty, staff, community, parents, and students are all stakeholders who share the responsibility of creating a community of life-long learners who will contribute effectively to the 21st century.

This mission statement would seem to indicate a powerful instructional setting. Certainly in my return to the high school classroom, I lobbied for a lively, edgy classroom, and when I outlined this to the students beforehand in my visits to Live Oak in previous semesters, I thought I had received students' tacit approval. At that point, I believed we, the students and I, had agreed on what mattered most and shared some of the same values and some of the kind of high ideals outlined in the Live Oak mission statement. And possibly we had—until the details and the specifics of the class emerged in daily work. What happened then was consistent: Students used their power from school regulations and parents to delay assignments, refuse assignments, and decline to venture farther in classroom work and discussion than they were accustomed. We never made a treaty; that caused friction throughout the semester and left, for many students, a lingering sense of unwillingness to compromise.

HIGH-STAKES TESTING

Along with concerns regarding treaties and content control, teachers and students face another set of realities that directly affects Live Oak High School and most comprehensive high schools in this country. Michie (2005) calls them "grim system realities" (p. 183), and they are prominent on the landscape of American public high schools.

One major issue is the inescapable emphasis on high-stakes testing. It permeates the school districts of my state—as it does in many states in the nation—and it was not just accident that close to the first thing that the principal Ms. Wood told me was that I could do virtually anything in Trailer 11 and with the 22 students—as long as they passed the state test. I heard this message clearly and, beyond the obvious obligation I had to help students with the two-part test, I also knew that if the students did not do well, it would be a message of sorts about university professors who return to high school settings. There was much at stake, of course for the students, but also for me.

In my previous years teaching high school, there was no high-stakes test from the school district or the state. Testing was largely a departmental or even an individual teacher and classroom matter. My unit or end-of-course tests were not reviewed or regulated, nor was my use of weighting of assignments in final grades. (On the other hand, in one high school where I taught, final semester grades were routinely altered without teacher knowledge or input to maintain a "balance" of scores.) Also, although I started the Advanced Placement (AP) program in English in the second high school where I taught, the emphasis on the final AP test, though considerable, paled in comparison to what I experienced with the statewide testing my 22 students faced.

Once in the classroom and with my Live Oak students, however, I had to confront in a very personal way just what I would do with these two high-stakes tests and how I would prepare the students. I worked to put together review materials for both tests and to set aside class time to practice, discuss, and, yes, review. Surprisingly, I also found that my students were not the least interested in my articulated beliefs about the narrowness and unreality of tests, views that I wanted to emphasize to them because I wanted to outline a clear distinction between political reality—the test—and what I considered the real learning of our class. Yet, for the students, test-taking was familiar territory, and their behavior showed me that they knew well and precisely how they needed to perform. As noted previously, the 22 students not only co-operated fully with the reviews, but they seemed to enjoy the direct and specific kind of question-and-answer format that the multiple-choice queries dictated. Student interest was avid, and the class review time was focused. And when the tests actually came, the students worked diligently during their administration and, to a person, performed well. For its part, Live Oak High School made a concerted effort to reward students who had scored appropriately by exempting them from later semester tests and providing school-wide recognition for those who made exceptionally high scores.

An unintended consequence, however, was students' full under-standing of the centrality of the tests and their truly logical unwilling-ness to continue working in any class after the tests had been given and the scores publicized. Only my persistence and the lure of the young adult novels and activities saved this last part of the semester; students who knew the importance of the state tests knew that when the scores were in the bag, the teaching year was over. This kind of reaction was understandable, but also, from a wider perspective, deadening. When a state test dominates teaching and learning and even student moti-vation, the balance of the school year can be skewed.

THE SCHEDULE OF THE SCHOOL DAY

I cannot present any hard evidence from my first high school teaching experiences to provide an irrefutable comparison, but my impression going back into high school teaching was that the schedule of the day and the interruptions of classes were far more persistently intrusive than I remembered. It was never clear what the week might hold re-garding changes in class length or pattern. In addition, my classroom at Live Oak was wholly porous: Students came and went into Trailer 11 almost at will; notes or appointments or other activities that took students out for all or some of the teaching period were routine and rarely cleared beforehand. This was considered acceptable. It was the norm for Live Oak High School culture, and the only real adjustment had to be on the part of the individual teacher.

This kind of intrusion was not really foreign to me, but I came to see the issue from an updated perspective. Mandated time in the class for school-related announcements—such as the time teachers were requested to distribute upcoming prom activities/pictures offers/rental packages—was considered important enough to usurp instructional time. The writing of appreciation notes to favorite teachers as a part of a school-wide/PTA project was also simply announced one day and required to be completed in our class and transmitted to the central office the next. English class, as always, was the place where the guidance counselors came to disseminate information; in my experience at Live Oak, the guidance counselor took far longer than promised, and it resulted in yet another syllabus/schedule change. Additionally, just as in my previous high school experiences, but with an updated face here, safety and fire drills and assorted assemblies were announced bare hours before required participation. For a variety of reasons that were never successfully explained, the statewide testing at Live Oak was rescheduled at least three times for both of the two-part administrations, necessitating juggling of assignments, deadlines, and other tests.

It made scheduling and preparing dauntingly tentative. It eroded a sense of rhythm and any kind of logical adherence to a plan. The schedule of the school day was not reasonable when I first began teaching— and far different from college and university classes that are considered essentially sacrosanct and are never interrupted and rarely suspended. Today, the school day is similarly unpredictable, and its variable schedule is not consistently conducive to an atmosphere of learning.

SCHOOL REGULATIONS

Perhaps this has never changed, but after years of teaching in a university environment where professors are autonomous and tenured professors are protected, it was instructive to return to an institution where the principal had total sway and where, in disputes, parents and students invoked school regulations by heart, and all must yield.

With barely a nod of the head, the principal at Live Oak ruled that a student project could not be viewed in class by other students: in the case of my students' video of "A & P," it could not, like all the other videos, be shared in class for group evaluation and discussion and thus had to be graded by myself alone.

Parents were fully empowered to demand immediate meetings with the principal regarding any teacher's classroom deadlines and assignments, and conferring first with the teacher was rarely necessary and not even expected. If any kind of violation or interpretation of school regulations appeared to be involved, *"I know my rights"* was invoked. Common sense and prior discussion with students or notification regarding syllabus details, as with the research paper draft deadlines, made little difference; school regulations appeared monolithic and could not be changed.

This is beyond the individual context of Live Oak: In an article in *English Leadership Quarterly*, a high school teacher in Rhode Island, Ronald T. Sion (2006), worries that "the system is creating a generation of young people who are all too familiar with how the [rules] may be manipulated in their favor" (p. 12). Sion concludes—and possibly many classroom teachers would concur: "Do not ask a teacher to be responsible for the student's share of the pie. . . . [it] feeds into irresponsibility" (p. 12).

For my part, I did not recognize soon enough the intersection of the Live Oak regulations and my class deadlines and assignments. Until I was in the situation, I could not grasp the implications of the school district policy on absenteeism and make-up work. Students had asked me if I would accept late work, and, not appreciating the issue, I replied "yes." What that meant was that late work could drag on and on and on. The initial power was in the parental excuse slip and the ensuing regulation six class days that students had to make up work. This was not part of my early high school teaching experience and not part of my work at the university: Many high schools, however, have similar regulations in place, and they can disrupt any pace and change the pattern of any class. I failed to see this clearly early on, and while I adjusted during the semester, it meant that tight deadlines—and elaborate, multipart projects such as the research paper, which involved successive drafts and responses to drafts—were doomed to failure. One excused absence (and I never had a parent *not* write such a note for an absence) and students were over a week behind.

In the second high school where I taught years ago, deadlines and assignments were necessarily rigid; we were on a course elective system and, insane as it sounds today, we changed courses and students every six weeks. I taught, one year, two dozen different elective courses to almost 400 different students. While the elaborate curricular plan of this particular school was, at the time, cracking under its own weight, and students were becoming truly resistant to the elective pattern and the constant change (and teachers were exhausted with the scheduling), most students knew that they needed to follow instructions and deadlines from day one. This was not true so many years later at Live Oak, and the school regulations regarding absences and make-up work did little but unravel instructional plans.

LOCUS OF CONTROL

Because high school is and remains an authoritarian, hierarchical culture, many high school students do not logically see themselves as taking control of their own lives and, when invited to do so in an instructional setting, many often decline the offer. I lived this clearly in my return to high school teaching: Despite the multiple avenues of communication regarding assignments and deadlines (paper copies, electronic copies, oral reminders, class postings, and communications by e-mail), my Live Oak students routinely misunderstood/forgot/ could not complete required work. It was similarly telling that my students rarely appeared chagrined about this fact or concerned about the consequences; the culture of the school dictated that they did not have to assume much individual responsibility and that the teacher should accept this and adjust.

My utterly overwrought response to Latosha (see Chapter 4) was part of my reaction to this reality: *I* was the one who did not accept this kind of evasion as an accepted tactic. Because there was apparently little at stake, it appeared to Latosha—and possibly to others in Trailer 11—that ignoring me was far easier than confronting the situation. This shift of responsibility also extended to the parents of my students. Talking with Alex's mother about his true disinclination to do academic work, her response was that that it was wholly the school's responsibility. She was waiting for *us* to find the solution and make it right for her talented but disengaged son. She was pointed and specific with me when we talked on the phone: When were *we* going to do something?

With the aborted field trip, it was clear, at least from Neal's comments, that the burden should not be shouldered by the students, but by the responsible adult: *I* could salvage the event if only *I* were not so unwilling to call every parent for the missing permission slips and make duplicate plans in case the last-minute calling did not work.

Essentially, what I had always referred to in my previous high school teaching as "let's make a deal" was not a reality in my Live Oak classroom. My urban students decades before had loudly demanded compromise, and that got my attention: I wrote learning contracts, gave multiple options, made sure that the negotiations were ongoing so that students stayed in class and stayed on task. But in Trailer 11, I felt I had negotiated beforehand with the students, outlining content and giving them options in almost all assignments and drawing from their comments, their selections, and work for the content of the all-important final tests. From my perspective, the whole class was student-centered and therefore should have been more successful.

But that was not the students' perspective. Although my students at Live Oak did not get concerned enough to explicitly demand change (other than extensions of deadlines and stopping all work at the end of the semester), many of them were having none of it as they experienced the class. As Larry Cuban (1993) observes in *How Teachers Taught*, "it is the students who ultimately consent to be managed" (p. 269). Some students simply took a passive-aggressive tack and in that way showed their uninterest. And I was not willing, ultimately, to adjust. I believed so strongly that what had been assented to in the outlined curriculum was set, and that the methodology and its variety would lure. Neither was true.

In Michael Apple's (1985) *Education and Power,* Apple discusses *Learning to Labour* (Willis, 1977), a British ethnography that looks at class and schooling and student resistance to the dominant ideology. Using primarily social studies teachers, Linda McNeil (1986) in *Contradictions of Control* looked at limitations on content and the essential anti-intellectual aspect of much of school, a setting where, she notes, teachers and students agree not to ask very much of each other.

As argued before, both of these studies—especially McNeil's—were influential as I contemplated what had happened in my class. For me, student resistance and the explicit way that students and teachers can often dance around each other, doing no harm but not engaging either, were deep concerns. Also important was the context of this large, suburban school. Although she worked in a very different setting, a progressive school in New York City, what Elizabeth Gold (2003) writes in *Brief Intervals of Horrible Sanity* could equally well be said of Live Oak, this large, suburban school:

> Schools don't exist separately from our culture. They *are* our culture. They reflect what we value, disdain, honor, ignore. The *madrasa* belongs to one world. And the American school—be it public or private, urban or suburban or rural—belongs to us, and tells our stories. (p. 323)

Live Oak High School and Trailer 11 were telling a story. The students did not feel engaged there, and whatever ownership of the class was offered, it was declined. This was not the students' class—the locus of control was somewhere else.

THE FICTION OF EXCELLENCE

Regardless of the level of classroom engagement, at Live Oak High School both parents and students had absorbed the language of rigor and excellence, and they were specific about demanding what they perceived was the best from the school. The problem came when the best could occasionally mean intense effort or the awarding of an assessment that was less than an "A." Then often the parents and students often cried foul, and the school hierarchy, in an effort to keep everyone appeased, mollified and bent. Far better, it appeared, to pass or graduate young people who think they have experienced rigor than to really expose them to same. This is one of the real issues in American high schools and, from my experience, also at Live Oak. Essentially, when students have been repeatedly told that they are superior, balancing demands and achievement benchmarks is difficult at best.

Recent studies confirm that many high school students and graduates believe that they are prepared for more challenging work, yet college professors think not. High school students surveyed through Indiana University's High School Survey of Student Engagement reported that 90,000 students from 28 states "come to class prepared with relatively little effort . . . devote little time to studying, yet still receive good grades" (Alliance, May 23, 2005, p. 7). Another survey sponsored by the National Governors Association found that "most of American's high school students believe they are adequately prepared" (Alliance, May 9, 2005, p. 7) but "approximately 1 in every 3 college freshmen takes a remedial course in college" because they "did not acquire the basic skills necessary" (Alliance, September 5, 2006, p. 1). Although basic skills were not an issue in my class, the students and I did not agree regarding responsibility, effort, and level of excellence; what I expected and what they were prepared to do widely differed.

IT WILL BE DIFFERENT IN COLLEGE

Among the 22 juniors in Trailer 11, there was an unspoken yet widespread belief that high school was mostly a way station, but that college, the golden ideal, would be far different. From my perspective, however, the students showed no real understanding of what college or college life would entail. In addition, many of them seemed to hold unrealistic expectations about college admissions, certainly based on their performance in high school.

One example was the senior student Alice, a bright young woman who had already been accepted into a state university when she began our class. I wondered if Alice's secured college admission provided an explanation for her behavior as she did not wish to follow assignment regulations, would not consult with me regarding projects, and would not revise any work. Perhaps for Alice there was the belief that college would never subject her to the kind of onerous requirements she was clearly confronting in Trailer 11. Another instance was Susan, who kept her head down on her desk for much of the semester and earned grades of D and C–. Susan's mother noted and Susan herself wrote and believed that once she got to college—for her, the goal was a specific Deep South university—all would be better. Susan never connected her own high school performance to college admissions or her ability to do university-level work once there. A third instance was LaBelle, who would consistently miss deadlines and was the first student post–state test to announce that she would no longer complete any work for the semester. LaBelle, of course, had requested my recommendation for college admission and expected to do well in college. However, I think she did not see any connection between her work and her attitude and what I might write to an admissions officer, as well as how she might fare two years from now.

If anyone, *I*, a university professor teaching this high school class, should have been a representative of college rigor and work. Some students observed in their opening notes to me that that is what they expected—and, unintentionally, this may well be much of what I provided in class, especially regarding independent work and deadlines—yet many of my students were absolutely unable to meet the challenge. It may be different in college, but surely completing work in high school and learning how to meet deadlines and expectations is a necessary prerequisite.

From where does this focus on college come? It is, for many, students and parents, the central goal of K–12 schooling, the prize at the end of the race. And while today's popular press is replete with statistics regarding rising university tuition costs, there are similarly numbers of articles touting the lifetime financial benefits of a college education. High school, for many, has only one legitimate goal: admittance to the college of choice. Thus, as Thomas Hine (1999) notes, colleges are "arbiters of what a high school ought to be (p. 153)," an influence that may not be appropriate but which is inescapable:

> Over the last 125 years [colleges] have . . . had a greater influence [on high schools] than such other powerful constituencies as business, labor, or even high school teachers and administrators . . . the quality of a high school is usually judged by its graduates' admission into and performance in college. Preparing students for life is an admirable goal, but you have to wait a lifetime to see whether you have done a good job. College admission, by contrast, is an immediate indicator of success. (p. 154)

Be that as it may, there is clear disconnect between what is required in many high schools and what is expected in college, and many students, such as mine at Live Oak, do not have a clue.

UNIVERSITIES AND SCHOOLS

At the time of my return to high school teaching, I was working with my own graduate students who were student teaching during that spring. For the first time in my work in teacher education, my graduate students and I were very much in similar situations, and the irony was not lost on me. We met once a week in a seminar on the university campus to share readings and journal entries, to discuss how things were going, and to talk teaching. All of us read from our journals to guide much of the discussion. I talked frankly about my concerns regarding my teaching and shared some of my preliminary writing on the topic. Empathetic and kind, my graduate students had little specific advice to offer. Their sympathy, however, was powerful. Novice teachers themselves, my students gave me a renewed sense of the teaching journey as a shared experience, even though at times it felt more like a shared commiseration.

And I continued to read along the way. One of the books I delved into was Sonia Nieto's (2003) *What Keeps Teachers Going?*, a study and description of how teachers stay in the urban classroom and continue to thrive. For Nieto, there are a variety of reasons teachers continue on: Among others, they remember and draw on why they came into the classroom (teaching as autobiography); they care for their students (teaching as love); they believe in the future (teaching as hope and possibility, or teaching as shaping futures). Some love their subject matter (teaching as intellectual inquiry), and some concentrate on social justice (teaching as democratic practice). Nieto also writes about teaching as anger and desperation, but she discusses clearly how we must contextualize best practice. Her comments strike me as important, especially in the light of my parallel work at Live Oak High School and with novice teachers in a school of education. Nieto cautions:

> [T]eacher preparation needs to shift its focus from questions of *what* and *how* to also consider questions of *why*. That is, the emphasis of some teacher

> education programs on strategies and techniques does little to prepare teach-
> ers to understand that these are just a small part of teaching . . . teaching is
> far more than specific procedures; it is a way of thinking about learning,
> and of one's students, of what will be most useful for them. (pp. 124–125)

I do think, looking back, that it is clearer to me than ever that most
all of us who work in teacher preparation need to revisit the classroom
and to teach in secondary school for an extended period of time. Whether
startling or confirmatory, teaching in a high school classroom can provide new insights and strong reminders of principles, limitations, and
issues that are unavoidable in secondary teaching.

Although schools of education supposedly encourage professors
to move from the academy back into the school, there are few real supportive structures and incentives for this kind of exchange. At the time
of my work at Live Oak High School, the only such structure in place
involved a teacher-in-residence program for classroom teachers who
would spend a year instructing university courses. The reciprocal route
was not so easily accomplished: My position at Live Oak was created
almost totally ad hoc and was, both from the school's and the university's perspective, something wholly optional on my part. I cannot
think that this should remain the standard. Universities and schools
need to link more frequently and more systematically, and have what
Alexander (2004) insists should be a "very real sense of connection"
(p. 623). Teaching needs to be shared across school boundaries.

WALKING OUR TALK

Despite all the factors explored previously, there is one more to consider: the individual teacher. It's interesting to contemplate that a content-
motivated, focused, and intentional teacher could not truly engage
22 students at Live Oak High School. I tried to walk my talk, as Susan
Hynds and Deborah Appleman (1997) detail, but it was not the success I had initially envisioned and worked for. Not only did I battle
unsuccessfully with certain characteristics of school and school culture, but I also became the teacher behind what Nancie Atwell (1985)
metaphorically calls her "big desk." I was the teacher who really had a

vision, a plan, an idea, and who dragged the students behind her. Atwell satirizes herself—and shows how the plan, the vision, the idea came to dominate, not the students. This pitfall I knew; but somehow I wonder if I didn't fall right into it in my return to high school teaching.

Falling in love with your plan, your scheme, can be a recipe for disaster and disappointment, and of all the characteristics one might give my work in Live Oak High School, I think this is closest to what I actually did. Despite the many choices I offered to students during the semester, despite the early cheerleading and the effort to get students to participate and direct the planning, it seems clear in retrospect that for a variety of reasons the work was never truly *owned* by most of the students and was, in way, never consented to. From an outside perspective it may well appear that I asked the students what they wanted, they replied politely and as best they could, and I went on and planned, while ignoring the resistance and difficulty that quickly escalated. Compared to what they were used to from other teachers, the plan or the class was too tight, too scripted, too set, and some students may have felt strangled by the syllabi, deadlines, and regulations. Certainly the failed field trip may well have been the climax of student resistance; while students ostensibly were interested in the Socratic Seminar and in collaborating with students from another school, it was clear that by not turning in the permission slips, half the class decided not to participate.

I did feel the bad vibrations that reverberated through the class, but I wasn't sure how to respond. Although there was not much that I as an individual teacher could do to make Sharonda and Jackie friends or to get most of the class to even look at and talk to Lee, much less like her, or to intervene when Sharon and Erin's general scorn of everyone in the class became too toxic, I wonder if I could have successfully intervened in discussions and small-group work and talked more explicitly about how and why we interact. I will never know if such tactics would have worked, but doubtless there were opportunities I missed, and I think I paid for those misses, as well as others, all during the semester.

But Trailer 11 is one class and one semester, and one teacher's journey. There are far wider implications for the future of American high schools and American public education. Let us look at the larger questions raised by my experience, and implications for the future of teaching in high schools.

12

WHAT WE MIGHT DO
IN THE FUTURE

To the extent that we embrace that challenge and the fundamental American philosophy behind it—that a free and powerful education is the absolute right of every citizen and that this education must be first and foremost seen as the mainspring of a democratic community—we can be hopeful.

—Theodore R. Sizer, *Horace's Hope* (1996, p. 147)

It has been some time since I ended my last class at Live Oak High School, but I am, in many ways, still there. It is much on my mind, and the experience of working in a community where the purpose of education is in dispute remains to me a troubling one. At Live Oak High School, the course content and the form of instruction did not inspire consistent student engagement, and I feel the loss keenly. Certainly conflict is part of any human enterprise, but it particularly undermines education, which is rooted in hope and the perhaps idealistic belief that teachers and students can connect in a way that fosters learning and growth.

It is arguable that it is futile to generalize from Live Oak High School and Trailer 11 outward: that one semester with one teacher and 22 students is not much beyond an individual event that can only be seen, if not explained, through a narrow lens. But my reading and my experience lead me to conclude that the work I did at Live Oak is not inconsistent with much of what is going on in many American high schools today.

For my students—mostly healthy, drug-free, suburban, middle-class, and largely well-supported by concerned parents—intellectual

interest and industry were spotty at best. Given choice and responsibility, most declined to become engaged. The treaties to which they
were accustomed in their high school experience were not enacted in
our class, and for some, that necessitated withdrawal and resistance.
For many of my students' parents, what mattered was the maintenance
of order and the fiction of excellence, and when the rules of the classroom seemed to change—when deadlines mattered, absences became
crucial, and grades might be involved—they intervened and protested.

For Live Oak High School, represented through its principal, Ms.
Wood, what mattered, at least for this year of this class, were the results of the state test; little else was important in classroom instruction
as long as that hurdle was successfully cleared.

For me, the teacher, what mattered most was that my students
learned, stretched, and truly grappled with the reading and with their
response in writing and talking. I wanted exploration, intellectual engagement, and an effort toward a standard of excellence. I had never
felt conflict was insurmountable, but the frequent, deadening disengagement I experienced was something else entirely.

In sum, my students were accustomed to a far different form of
engagement and a far different definition of learning. Despite their
initial assent and control over much of the class, the students did not,
as Deborah Meier (1995) writes, see themselves as "parties to their own
education" (p. 163), and they acted accordingly. For the parents, student satisfaction and good grades mattered. For the school, maintenance of the system and passing of the tests were paramount.

HOW DID WE GET HERE?

Educational history gives us some insight. In 1892, a debate regarding
high school occurred when the National Education Association sponsored what came to be known as the Report of the Committee of Ten.
The group was charged with standardizing the high school curriculum and was concerned that high school courses were taught differently depending on whether students were going to college or not. The
Committee of Ten also found that, in particular, English language arts
courses were not being geared to two basic needs: developing commu-

nication skills and cultivating a taste for reading. A few years later, in 1918, the significantly more influential *Cardinal Principles* report (Commission, 1918) advocated the establishment of large, comprehensive high schools where all students would attend and where English would include "studies of direct value," relating theory and student experience. In particular, the authors of the report advocated that the curriculum include topics beyond the academic, and they lobbied for attention to certain principles: health, command of fundamental processes, worthy home membership (today's consumer education), vocation, citizenship, worthy use of leisure time, and ethical character. Though the language of this list seems quaint today, the intent rings clear: Students needed to learn more in school than traditional subject matter, and life skills and quality of life were also important.

The *Cardinal Principles* was influential, and the interest in preparing students for life became a major tenet of an encompassing concept called the Progressive Movement. The movement's most influential proponent was the legendary writer and educational theorist John Dewey (1916/1961), and the movement started formally in 1919 with the founding of the Progressive Education Association and did not truly fade until the 1950s.

For the Progressive Movement, the real needs of students were of great import, and in language arts the 1935 publication *An Experience Curriculum in English* outlined how to meet student interests in a realistic course of studies. The curriculum seemed successful; research involving 240 schools and 3,600 students, called the Eight-Year Study, (Aikin, 1942) confirmed that students whose classes were built around problems and issues that concerned them—problems that involved the family and the community, not just the classroom—did as well in college as their more traditionally educated counterparts. The compelling nature of the Progressive Movement's ideas is enduring, even today, and echoes of its tenets are found in many contemporary books about American education. Nevertheless, the curricular design advocated by the Progressive Movement was not widely adopted by high schools across the country.

The debate shifted sharply, however, with launching of the Russian satellite Sputnik in 1957. Sputnik seemed to represent the failure of American society and the waning of American political dominance, and it caused a panic of sorts. Sputnik fueled a concern that American students were falling behind, especially in relation to young people in other countries. High schools were seen as crucial in ensuring American world competitiveness, and the institution of the National Defense Education Act (NDEA) ensured that the "most able" high school students would be exposed to an academic curriculum that included more attention to mathematics, foreign language, and the sciences.

In was in this atmosphere that James Bryant Conant (1959), former president of Harvard, wrote *The American High School Today* in which he outlined how the comprehensive high school could truly serve democracy and American society. However, Conant's vision, and also that of others who saw the comprehensive high school as part of American national defense, was usurped in the late 1960s and 1970s. The civil rights movement, the feminist movement, the furor over the Vietnam War, and the revelations of the Watergate scandal profoundly affected American society; schools attempted to respond to changes and pressures regarding poverty and race and other social issues. Indeed, many students had not reacted positively to the academic curriculum post-Sputnik. In an effort to meet student needs, to capture interest, and ensure graduation, high school curricula attempted a more personal and flexible course of studies than the traditionally academic one envisioned by previous generations. The thinking regarding high school cycled back historically: High schools would, once again, prepare students not just for college but also for contemporary life.

In 1983, though, high school was seen as preparing for nothing much at all; the influential *A Nation at Risk* (U.S. Department of Education, 1983) decried the high school as wholly failing and maintained that "we have even squandered the gains in student achievement made in the wake of the Sputnik challenge" (p. 1). The average achievement of high school students was a focus; *Risk* maintained that it was "lower than 26 years ago when Sputnik was launched" (p. 3). The report was dramatic and emphatic, widely read and widely believed. The "rising tide of mediocrity" (p. 1) that it envisioned was shocking to many and renewed concerns about the quality and focus of American education. Although over 20 years have passed since the publication of *Risk*, high schools remain a topic of criticism and reform efforts, and the warnings of *A Nation at Risk* are today still quoted.

CONTEMPORARY CONCERNS

Currently we do not face the same issues of the late 19th and 20th centuries, but high school as an institution and its function in preparing for life and preparing for college endures as a topic of debate. "High school needs to be more than just the end point of the K–12 system" (p. 93), Martinez and Bray (2002) contend in *All Over the Map*. Indeed, while efforts to innovate and streamline elementary and middle-level education have been ongoing for some years, the high school has yet to join the movement. Martinez and Bray speculate:

> Academic gains at the elementary school level can be tentatively linked to policy action in the past decade; increased funding, more widespread preschool for the disadvantaged, new attention to reading, smaller class sizes in grades K–3, and the development of standards and accountability systems. However, few states have tackled high school policy issues so comprehensively, and the potential levers for improvement are not obvious. (p. 5)

At the 2004 National High School Summit, National Governors Association chairman Mark Warner reiterated the conclusion above, noting that "the assumption that fixing the early grades would somehow magically fix high schools has not borne out." And while contemporary polls call for high school reform, there have been no recent studies of high school on the scale of those conducted by the educational researchers of past decades, studies that were comprehensive, well-researched, and highly influential. Those studies include those of James Bryant Conant (*The American High School Today*, 1959 and *The Comprehensive High School*, 1967), Ernest L. Boyer (*High School*, 1983), John I. Goodlad (*A Place Called School*, 1984), Arthur G. Powell, Eleanor Farrar, and David K. Cohen (*The Shopping Mall High School*, 1985), and Theodore R. Sizer (the three-volume *Horace* series, 1984, 1992, 1996).

Most of these studies are about twenty-five years old, a very long time in educational research; the remarkable aspect of these books is not only the fact that they have not been replicated but that they are still salient in the early 21st century. Today, as before, the high school tries to do too much and ends up doing little well. "We want it all" (p. 33) wrote John I. Goodlad in 1984 in his critique of the vision of the comprehensive high school; that this underlying problem still exists is something that few educational communities would today deny. Further, calls for change and reform remain largely unanswered or, at the worst, answered through calls for more testing.

REFORM MODELS AND SCHOOLS

Recent examinations of high school reform offer little consolation. As one contemporary article observes (Toch, Jerald, and Dillon, 2007), "The high school reform movement resembles a sprawling 19th-century Russian novel, with dozens of actors and innumerable initiatives" (p. 434). A 1994 study that surveyed more than 10,000 high schools (and received responses from about 3,000) regarding restructuring efforts concluded that little had changed in response to the calls for reform. Educational researcher Gordon Cawelti (1994) observed that "the rate of change in the nation's high schools overall is highly variable . . . the traditional institution remains dominant" (n.p.). Similarly, Martinez and Bray asserted in 2002 that "if students show up, can pass their courses, and do not cause trouble, they will still graduate . . . findings of 20 years ago are still true (p. 1)."

Currently, in the name of a rigor that has been seen as lacking in high schools, there is in almost every state a reliance on the efficacy of large-scale high-stakes testing. The successful negotiation of these tests determines student graduation or, in some states, the kind of diploma granted upon graduation. And if test-them-to-death will not work to ensure rigor, some high school reformers have embraced a call to eliminate the last, possibly redundant year of high school, supposedly solving part of the "problem" by reducing the number of years in the secondary school setting. Another approach is increasing the use of dual credit enrollment, where courses taught in high school are used for college credit. This kind of curriculum reconsideration embraces a strengthening interest in International Baccalaureate (IB) programs, a curriculum that is appealing to some teachers and students. The more widespread Advanced Placement (AP) programs—though not without their critics—are also seen by many as "more difficult than 'regular' high school courses and thus . . . a proxy for rigorous and challenging curriculum" (Martinez and Bray, 2002, p. 12), and are also part of a possible curricular reform.

But will any of these address the major issues confronting high school curriculum and structure? Will they, if implemented, change high schools? Harvey Daniels, Marilyn Bizar, and Steven Zemelman's (2001) *Rethinking High School: Best Practice in Teaching, Learning, and Leadership* observes that "most American high schools still look pretty much the way they did when the milestone *A Nation at Risk* report was released in 1983 and, for that matter, how they looked in 1923" (p. 19). Further, Daniels, Bizar, and Zemelman write:

> As institutions, high schools are profoundly, frustratingly intractable. They seem to shrug off all criticisms, squirm out from under all indictments, and repel all change. In order to document any significant improvement in American high schools at all, we are forced to look back across many decades . . . [it is a] slow system! (pp. 19–20)

In an essay, educational writer and teacher Thomas Newkirk (2003) concurs:

> There is an image of high school that is embedded in the minds of all who went through them; it has a particular architecture, a system of bells, seating charts, wall posters, subjects, tests, grades, proms, athletic events, that is both maddeningly and reassuringly familiar. For all the criticism of schools, the public is quite resistant to major tampering with this picture. . . . Yet it is a system where a majority of students fail to develop the habits of mind central to reflective thought. (p. 402)

Although this is not true of all high schools and their students, it is true of many, and it is part of my experience at Live Oak.

Coalition of Essential Schools

The assessments explored above are mostly negative, but it is not because no one has tried; there have been many significant reform efforts. One of the most intriguing is the innovative Coalition of Essential Schools (CES), a model begun in 1984 by Ted Sizer that uses small school units and courses of studies that are multidisciplinary. Teachers in Coalition schools would not be narrow, discipline-oriented instructors but ones whose interdisciplinary teaching would open the traditional confines of the high school curriculum into broader configurations. The Coalition plan is based on principles, not a prescribed model; Coalition schools also address assessment by focusing not on test scores per se but on actual student "demonstrations of mastery." Among its 10 principles, the Coalition holds:

- The central goal of schooling is intellectual development.
- Students should study a few essential areas deeply.
- High expectations should be held for everyone.
- Learning environments should be personalized.
- Students should be constructing meaning rather than being filled up with information.
- Teachers should act as coaches and guides.
- The key outcome is not test scores but what students can actually do.

The inventive schema, though, has not become widely adopted. While approximately 400 CES high schools exist today (Bergeson & Heuschel, 2006, p. 146), as a large-scale model for reform, Coalition schools are not widespread.

Founder Ted Sizer (1996) understands well the challenge of reforming high schools, and outlines it in *Horace's Hope*:

> The ways in which high schools are organized and resources are distributed make serious teaching virtually impossible even for devoted and experienced teachers . . . the "world-class standard," so easily set, is utterly unattainable in schools as they are currently structured. (p. 67)

That said, it is still daunting to make changes. Sizer (1996), like many others who have studied the issue and worked for change, echoes the challenges of reform:

> The stability in public education comes from the extraordinary inertia of traditional practice. Pressure for change, whether wise or unwise, ultimately emerges as hiccups . . . [which leave] the schools' design and routines much as they are now. (p. xv)

Nevertheless, there are examples of high schools that embody reform principles, and two are worthy of note.

Central Park East and Best Practices High School

Central Park East Secondary School in New York and Best Practices High School in Chicago have attempted to embody reform. Central Park East, whose principal was the gifted Deborah Meier (1995), is "probably the best known" of the Coalition high schools (Bergeson and Heuschel, 2006, p. 147). Meier detailed her mid-1990s work in *The Power of Their Ideas: Lessons for America from a Small School in Harlem.* In that book she acknowledged squarely the difficulty of the endeavor:

> The obstacles that block the path of reforming a high school are harder to budge than those that face elementary schools. . . . The external demands for proof and evidence are far greater in high school, the rituals more fixed (curriculum, credit hours, course sequences, daily schedules), and the "next" institution—college or workplace—even less under our influence. But even these factors were not the most important.
>
> The big, mindless high school, no matter how dysfunctional, has many fans, including kids. When we talk with school officials and local politicians about restructuring large high schools, the first thing they worry about is what will happen to the basketball or baseball teams, the after-school program, and other sideshows; that the heart of the school, its capacity to educate, is missing, seems almost beside the point. (pp. 31–32)

Yet Central Park, although on a small scale, was able to implement many of the principles of the Coalition of Essential Schools.

Best Practices High School was born in the mid-1990s, and *Rethinking High School* (Daniels, Bizar, & Zemelman, 2001) is its story. Although not a member of the Coalition of Essential High Schools, Best Practices, like Central Park East, is characterized by innovative curriculum and a vision shared by teachers, students, and parents. Some of its tenets include flexible scheduling, small size, curriculum that is geared to inquiry in "topics that matter," student-centered teaching, and student input into in "all elements of school life" (pp. 10–11). But as of this writing, Best Practices High School, like those in the Coalition of Essential Schools, has not emerged as a persuasive or pervasive model for large-scale reform.

New American High Schools

And of course the federal government has entered into the arena. The U.S. Department of Education's New American High Schools (NAHS) initiative, though, has not made significant inroads into high school structure and is essentially defunct. Started in 1996 and funded in 2000 with $1.4 million, the 60 designated NAHS schools, according to the Department of Education, "differ from traditional high schools in many ways"—ways that are striking in that, if this is the "new" high school, something is terribly wrong with those currently in place. For instance, these new and innovative schools featured, among other qualities, high standards, teachers working together, strong principal leadership, a focus on student learning, and the use of technology to enhance achievement. The idea that these factors should be considered unusual seems, in and of itself, revealing, and may indicate the paucity of ideas regarding high school reform.

THE URGENCY OF THE ISSUE

There is no current Boyer or Conant or Sizer or Goodlad; there is no new Deborah Meier. But despite the lack of such seminal studies and new leaders with visions and reform models, there is no lack of urgency regarding the necessity for high school reform. Educator Anne C. Lewis (2004) writes in the *Phi Delta Kappan* that "what no one has is a lot of time" (p. 564):

> In case you haven't noticed, the traditional American public high school is on the chopping block . . . a sudden burst of talk, money, and policy proposals has made it obvious that those in high schools are going to have to act—and soon. (p. 563)

Microsoft CEO Bill Gates has called high school "obsolete" (Alliance, December 12, 2005, p. 1), and the Bill and Melinda Gates Foundation has earmarked $1 billion to study the issue and to sponsor work that may change large high schools into smaller ones. The concern about the size of high schools is appropriate, but, predictably, other current efforts seem less helpful. The 2004 *Ready or Not: Creating a High School Diploma That Counts* (sponsored by the American Diploma Project) is a case in point. The document's conclusions are hardly wide-ranging, and Lewis (2004) observes that *Ready or Not*:

> defines student success exclusively in terms of meeting high academic standards . . . all states would be working from the same set of standards [and all] students [will] undertake an honors curriculum. (p. 563)

In a similarly uninspired solution, President George Bush in his 2006 State of the Union address called for additional reading and math assessments at the high school level as if, in and of itself, more testing could be a solution to high school reform. Certainly money is not plentiful: The federal 2008 fiscal year budget proposal increases support for some high school programs (such as Advanced Placement) but, to pay for it, cuts other programs which benefit high schools (Alliance, February 5, 2007). And, despite the urgency of Lewis's call for reform, noted previously, in a subsequent 2007 editorial in the same journal, she terms the current reform efforts "sluggish" (p. 420).

ASSESSING THE IDEAS

In order to make the high school experience more pertinent, more intellectual, more challenging, we need to consider a number of possibilities beyond making the curriculum entirely an honors one and instituting additional testing. A number of approaches have been advanced in recent years; some very promising ones have yet to gather wide support, and many do not take high school seriously as a viable entity that can fill a unique educational and developmental function. In fact, many of the current proposals are based on the premise that if it is good for college, it is better for high school. Like my students in Trailer 11, who could only live for their future life on a college campus, not inhabit the disappointing present, some reformers can often envision nothing more sophisticated than making the time in high school shorter—so that the wait before college is reduced—and moving college-level kinds of work and study down into the high school.

This idealization of the college model absolutely avoids the issue that young people from age 14 to 18, living with parents or guardians in a home setting, might have some specific intellectual needs and developmental aspects that college freshmen may not have.

Be that as it may, the current proposals include:

Eliminate the Last Year of High School

If high school study is missing the mark, some reformers conclude that reducing its scope and length seems sensible. Many argue that senior year is a waste of time and a placeholder for many young people. Our nation's legislators often agree. At a 2005 House of Representatives hearing on high school reform in front of the Committee on Education and the Workforce, Representative Tom Osborne (R-NE) called the senior year "a wasteland" (U.S. House, p. 29). At the same hearing, Iowa Governor Tom Vilsack characterized the last year of high school as "a total waste. It is about the prom. It is about football. It is about everything but what it ought to be about" (p. 30). If indeed students like Alice and Susan do think that things will be better in college, this approach would change the rhythm of high school, accelerate and compress the curriculum, and graduate students at 17 after three years of more intense, and possibly higher-stakes studies.

But this option is hardly inventive or generative: It simply compresses four years of study into three and puts even younger students into college or into the workplace. If the high school curriculum and course of study needs restructure, lopping off 10 months can hardly address the complexity of the issues and leaves the basic work—reform and redirection—undone.

Mimic the Success of International Baccalaureate (IB) and Advanced Placement (AP) Programs

While IB is seen by many as elitist, and some colleges are reassessing accepting for credit exam scores from AP courses (because students with exempting scores do not appear equipped to handle college-level work), some feel that these two programs often inspire more student engagement than the standard high school curriculum. Yet despite the recommendations of *Ready or Not*, not all students want to be designated as honors students—and some who are so designated, including many of my students at Live Oak High School, do not merit the designation by any measure of academic achievement. Because not all students wish to work in IB or AP settings, placing a large proportion of a student body into such programs makes little sense and may, indeed, cause many to find high school study even more alienating than before. Converting the high school curriculum to an all-IB or all-AP one is not realistic.

Encourage Dual Enrollment Courses

If, as many believe, the high school curriculum is inadequate, some conclude that a sensible approach is to allow students to take college courses while they are still in high school. These courses are intended both to address curricular rigor issues and to boost students' potential for college success.

There are arguments in favor of dual enrollment. Those who testified at the 2005 high school reform hearing in front of the House of Representatives Committee on Education and the Workforce were uniformly positive about dual enrollment. In addition, an eight-and-a-half-year longitudinal study released by the Department of Education concluded that "a challenging high school curriculum is the best pre-college predictor of whether a student will receive a bachelor's degree" (Alliance, February 21, 2006, p. 4) and indicated that the number of credits freshmen students have obtained by the end of their first year in college is positively correlated with college graduation. Dual enrollment, which has a history of some 20 years, could address both of these issues. Yet Martinez and Bray (2002) question the viability of dual enrollment as an approach to high school reform and also raise issues of access:

> Questions have been raised about the overlapping missions of high school and college and whether it makes sense for both to focus on the same cohort of students. Concerns about course quality, the easy transfer of credits and who should pay the college costs for dual enrollment are associated with some programs. Equal access to dual enrollment programs

for students in high poverty schools is also an important issue that should be considered. (p. 15)

High school is not the new college; dual enrollment does little to address curricular concerns at the high school level. Instead, dual enrollment uses college courses as a quick fix and ignores fundamental issues of secondary school curriculum reform and school structure.

Making high school into college is not the only model currently being discussed regarding the reform of high schools. Three other threads of reform, all of which are also pertinent, include:

Reconsider the Small Schools Movement

"Lost in the crowd" is a real factor for many high school students, and smaller schools can engender more engagement than those such as Live Oak with its 2,300 students. While "federal policy has fizzled out" (Lewis, 2007, p. 419) regarding the small schools movement, others are not so dismayed. The Gates Foundation is addressing this issue; Deborah Meier (1995) makes this case explicitly when she discusses her work with Central Park East Secondary School (p. 53); Ted Sizer's (1996) Coalition schools are also similarly small, the "human-scale places" (p. 91) he lauds in *Horace's Hope*. When high schools are limited in size, the potential for a true learning community becomes more real. As one recent study of secondary schools, *The High Schools We Need* (Bergeson & Heuschel, 2006) urges, "caring and personal environments" (p. 168) are essential to effective reform. Similarly, influential researcher Nel Noddings (1992) has insisted on the importance of personal attention, on the need for care in student learning and in school environments. Huge institutions struggle with issues of impersonality; to be effective for all, schools need to be smaller.

Work to Change the Negative Impact of Large-Scale, High-Stakes Testing

My students at Live Oak High School clearly understood the importance of the state test and while their performance was more than acceptable, the test also negatively affected their attitude toward their classes and toward their own commitment to continued work. Indeed, in *Contradictions of School Reform*, Linda M. McNeil (2000) worries about "the long-term effects of students whose entire educational experience is dominated by standardization" (p. 17). Larry Cuban (2001) also addresses also the chilling effect of testing:

> The impact of standards-based performance and accountability for test score improvement has hardened . . . traditional teaching practices. Once-flourishing progressive classroom approaches such as portfolios, project-based teaching and performance-based testing that blossomed between the mid-1980s and the early 1990s, for example, have since shriveled under the unrelenting pressure for higher test scores. (pp. 179–180)

If standardized tests and large-scale testing did not dominate the high school curriculum as they currently do, it is possible that what goes on in the classrooms may significantly change for the better. As Ted Sizer (1996) argues in *Horace's Hope*, "some teachers with classroom zest are profoundly undermined by testing systems that do not demand a comparable response from students" (pp. 95–96). In Trailer 11, the influence of the state test was almost overwhelming, making any kind of work beyond the test a struggle.

Address the Staggering Dropout Rate

It is estimated that three out of 10 high school students, or one million students a year, do not graduate. Some of this may well be attributable to high-stakes testing, but some of it may also be part of the high school structure and curriculum. Although none of my students at Live Oak was a possible dropout, the issue is an important one nationwide and, for some, indicates the failure of the high school to engage.

Why do students drop out? Teacher Lawrence A. Baines (2003) surveyed some 50 high school students regarding their daily life in school; through their journals, he and coauthor Gregory Kent Stanley found what they called "standards-based ennui" in high school. The students' accounts of their work were numbing—the students found high school "irrelevant, sterile, dull, or worse," and Baines and Kent urged teachers to remember that "a student must first be engaged before he or she can learn" (p. 168). The policy response of "more test-ing and stronger accountability" (p. 168) would never, the authors concluded, ameliorate what they called the "disengagement and loath-ing" of the students they surveyed in high school. These are students who, given the chance, are likely to drop out and, unless the high school changes in structure and design, this pattern may well continue.

AND AT THE END

And so the conversation and the debates and the plans continue as educators, policy makers, and legislators consider the shape of the high school. At the same time, however, teachers and students and adminis-trators continue with the daily work. In high schools all over the country bells ring, students change classes, the principal makes announcements, and cafeterias serve pizza and tater tots. We all, in school, go on. But we also need to reconsider, to stop and not go on. What matters most is the future, and education is essential to that future. When "good enough" becomes the standard of excellence, when the educational and wider community can accept as routine the kind of disengagement that was the norm in Trailer 11, then the promise of the American high school is unfulfilled.

Specifically, we need to consider the problems inherent in a struc-ture where students can and do refuse to work in their classes; where, in some settings, it is easy for them to do so without any negative ef-fects. We need to consider why students might not respond to the power of choice in their curriculum and why administrators might inadvertently make it easy for students to avoid challenging work. And, regarding the home setting, we need to consider why parents and guardians have so much power to dictate classroom practices and policies.

The answer to these questions is at the heart of what did and did not happen in Trailer 11. Essentially, many systems are not serving students and their parents and, in addition, are not giving teachers the kind of support they need. The status quo remains largely intact, but at the end, even before graduation day, we can question if anything of real merit has been accomplished in the schools.

This kind of questioning is an integral part of the teaching life, a life and a profession that is characterized by a very intense kind of introspection. To be successful and to be effective, teachers must constantly reexamine themselves, their practice, their relationship with and effect on students. They must engage in Shulman's (2000) scholarship of teaching and learning and the "practitioner research" self study explored by Borko, Liston, and Whitcomb (2007), which "examines practice from the inside" (p. 5). Despite the community aspect of instruction—work done in context and with and among many others—individual and reflective self-contemplation is a central part of teaching and an inescapable aspect of ongoing teacher renewal. And there is, even for those long beyond the narcissism of their own adolescent selves, a strong and important personal aspect of teaching. The success of the individual act of teaching remains particularly important to those who choose to stay in the classroom.

For me, returning to the high school classroom was a conscious and deliberate risk. I chose to go back to high school teaching because of curiosity and because of concerns about my own stagnation. At the beginning, I felt I was embarking upon a journey, a journey that would demand that I stretch as a teacher. During the semester I spent with my 22 students at Live Oak High School and after, I underwent serious self-examination. That work was consuming and at times difficult; brief as my return to high school teaching may have been, it impelled me for some time afterward to unpackage, examine, and assess.

These suburban young people of Trailer 11, children of relative affluence, were far different from the urban students I had first taught and who had made me a high school teacher so many years ago. Their life crises, as far as I could tell, were milder than those of my previous students, and their connection to and support by their parents were far stronger. They were not alienated from school or even English class, and their comfortable habitation in the school setting made my role far different from what it had been in my early career teaching. These students knew school and its boundaries and were confidently headed to college and a bright future. My students years before had hardly been that comfortable or cushioned, that assured, that confident. What I encountered in Trailer 11 was a different culture and a different set of expectations, and, for me, it was a struggle for much of the semester.

As teachers, we must be honest about our struggles, about our failures as well as successes. Tom Newkirk (1992) rails against teacher stories that are unremittingly upbeat:

> What I find most difficult to believe, the teacher never shows signs of despondency, frustration, anger, impatience, or disappointment. If there is anger or frustration, it is directed at external forces—administrators, testing services, the government . . . but never at themselves or their students. The teachers I read about don't doubt their competence, or at least they don't admit to their doubts. (p. 24)

I have to admit my doubts and also that I have learned and relearned some verities, a number of which affect my own ongoing work within a school of education. Among other things, I have relearned:

- That teaching is continual discovery; even for a veteran teacher, there is no plateau of skill or comfort to which we arrive that is permanent;
- That teaching is singularly hard when it appears that, for the students, the work is neither satisfying nor truly engaging;
- That the structure of school and school culture remains a powerful influence, and not always a positive one;
- That, despite all of the above, the work of teaching, the work of reading and talking and writing in the classroom, has power to make a difference in students' lives.

At the end, in spite of any disappointments or misplaced expectations, for me this last point trumps all others.

EPILOGUE

Since my time at Live Oak High School, the opening of a new high school in the school district has eased crowding, and all the trailers surrounding the main Live Oak building are now gone. Ms. Wood is still the principal, but Terry has become a new mother and has transferred to another high school. Kasey's media literacy program has become more successful and has expanded, and an entire wing of Live Oak now houses a video studio and additional classroom space. Kasey looks back on the group I taught and calls them an "anomaly"; she reports that those in the current media literacy group are far more harmonious and hardworking.

As for the 22 students in Trailer 11, about two-thirds entered college, and some are still enrolled. Although on different coasts, both Ellen Patton and Ashton are in film school. Neal, despite his learning disability, is studying in college to be a veterinarian, and Aaron, despite his tremendous academic talent, has failed out. Susan never made it to her Deep South university but is working at a day-care center, and Alex, whose mother was so exasperated with the school and his academic career, received a scholarship to play football at a small college. Ellen Wall, Sharon, and a few others are also enrolled in universities and appear to be doing well. Sharonda has been in fairly consistent touch by e-mail; she is majoring in journalism at a university, writing for a local paper, and her son is a healthy and well-adjusted toddler. As we have chatted online, she remembers our time and some of the projects positively but notes, "We as a class were tired of one another." As for her teacher, she speculates, "maybe you were too much for us to handle at the time."

Kasey tells me that my research paper project has become a staple for teachers at Live Oak, and, if I ever want to teach another class, she would love for me to come back. I'm thinking about it.

And, as I think about it, I return to a favorite article of mine, which is cited earlier in this account and that must, I think, end it. It is a tough meditation on the hard times of teaching and on what many of us in the classroom do not like to think much about—failure. I stubbornly hand out copies of this article even though most of my graduate students don't like to discuss what it says, don't like to think about its implications. It's not that I enjoy dwelling on the negative, but the truth of this article is striking. From my perspective, from my teaching life and the view from Trailer 11, Richard A. Hawley (1979) has it right, both in his description of the problem and in his solution:

> Failure—real failure—is palpable everywhere in the teaching process. We need to name it and to face it, so that we may continue. If we insulate

ourselves sufficiently with defenses, we may go unhurt, but we will teach nothing, while providing students models of flight and disengagement. Acknowledging failure and acknowledging defenses, we may come to know as much about our business as the medieval scholastics knew about God: what he is not and that he is necessary. Now off to class. (p. 600)

I take what wisdom I can find from my semester at Live Oak High School. Sometimes that wisdom is uplifting; sometimes it is nothing more than agreeing with T. S. Eliot in the *Four Quartets* that "For us, there is only the trying. /The rest is not our business" ("East Coker," 1943/1952, p. 128). I have worked to make things better throughout my teaching career—looking, like all hopeful teachers, to create and maintain a sustainable context for teaching and learning. Although I wonder if my work has influenced much beyond a small circle of teachers who have read my books and students who have taken my classes, my teacher's journey continues. The view from Trailer 11 is bittersweet, but I am grateful I am and plan to remain a teacher.

The work continues, the work is essential; so back to class I go.

Appendix A:
Research Paper Assignment
and Schedule
(Student Handout)

A. FAMILY HISTORY

This research paper details your family history and stories; primary sources (i.e., interviews with family members and use of family documents such as baby books, recipes, photographs, letters, etc.) are important to the success of this project. Because this project involves the privacy and experiences of people other than yourself, check with your family members before you agree to take on this research. Part of this paper can include: family origins (tracing the family to another continent or part of the country); autobiographical incidents and anecdotes; special family celebrations; ethnic maxims and proverbs; foods; distinct family experience and behavior; sketches of various family members; heroines and heroes of the family; "characters" in the family. This paper should also touch on the broader ethnic literature of the family, including folk tales, myths and legends, proverbs, historical fiction, nonfiction, films. What has influenced members of your family or what represents this family in literature and in film?

An appendix for this project can include interview transcripts, family trees, photographs, maps showing the movement of the family, memorabilia, correspondence, etc.

B. YOUR DATE OF BIRTH

Taking your date of birth as the starting point and focus, you will research that day from a number of perspectives: that of your family, the community where you were born, the nation, and the world. Because this project involves the privacy and experiences of people other than yourself, check with your family members before you agree to take on this research. First, for part one, you will need to interview family members who recall the date of your birth and the circumstances surrounding it. What do they remember and where were they at the time? Was there anything memorable or distinctive about your arrival and its circumstances? Who was there (other than your mother) when you were born? What does a baby book or records (such as a birth certificate) tell you? Second, for part two, you will need to use newspaper resources. If you can locate a copy of the local paper from the community where you were born, what was happening on your birth day? What was happening in the nation and the world (see the *Washington Post*, *New York Times*, *Los Angeles Times*)? Also for part two, you can do a global overview of this day, or you can concentrate on a single aspect of the day that, along with the details of your birth, interests you. This focus can include, for the day: politics, commerce (check the ads for houses, cars, clothes, appliances, etc.), movies, weather, sports scores, crime, art, etc.

C. LITERARY

I. An American Writer

Choose an American author of fiction, nonfiction, or poetry (or a journalist or humorist) and in a well-researched paper give an overview of his or her work, citing in detail at least five of his or her works, two of which you should have read in their entirety (only one of those works can be something you read previously for this class). What ideas and themes did this writer address; what techniques did the writer use; what responses were given to his or her work? What is important about reading this writer today? Do not concentrate on the biographical details but on the work of the writer, what it says, how it is assessed by others, and why it is significant.

2. Themes in American Literature

Choose a theme in American literature (the innocence of nature, the road, westward movement, reinventing the self, upward mobility, the aristocracy of merit, the wisdom of the working man/woman, loss of innocence in the city, corruption of industry, etc.) and sketch it through five works, two of which you should have read in their entirety (only one of those works can be something you read previously for this class). What makes this theme appealing or important to American literature and what do we learn about it from the literature? Is this theme still being addressed today? Why or why not? Note on literary topics above: it may be tempting to download papers on these topics and borrow others' work and words: Please resist this temptation. It is plagiarism and will result in a zero for the assignment.

D. CULTURAL TOUCHSTONES IN AMERICA

Choose something that is quintessentially American and research it thoroughly. Topics can include: baseball, football, basketball, Coke, motorcycles, rap and hip-hop, the hamburger, suburbia, the summer vacation, the cookout, Thanksgiving, the car, our national park system, the interstate highway, etc. Trace its history, including its origins, use, marketing, and, ultimately, its significance to American culture, and, possibly, to world culture.

E. OPEN (IF YOU HAVE OTHER IDEAS, SEE ME)

RESEARCH PAPER SCHEDULE

Preliminary Topic Discussion   February 1
Preliminary Topic Submitted   February 5
Preliminary Topic Approved   February 9
                    5 points

Final Topic Submitted   February 12
Final Topic Approved   February 16
                    5 points

Source List Submitted   February 22
Source List Approved   February 24
                    5 points

Source Notes Submitted   March 5
Source Notes Approved   March 9
                   10 points

Conference with Teacher   March 12–14
                    5 points

Draft 1 Submitted to Revision Group   March 19
                   10 points

Draft Revised
Draft 2 Submitted to Revision Group   March 23
                   10 points

Draft Revised
Draft 3 Submitted to Teacher   March 27
                   10 points

Draft Revised
     POINTS POSSIBLE   **60 POINTS**

Final Draft Submitted   April 3
    POINTS POSSIBLE   **40 POINTS**
    [Based on format, organization,
    and effective writing]

    TOTAL POINTS   **100 POINTS**

Appendix B:
Short Story Project:
Creating a Movie Trailer
(Student Handout)

Requirements

Length: One minute

Script: Submit rough draft for approval and final draft (typed, double-spaced with accurate directions re camera work) when trailer is viewed

Participation: All students in short-story group must contribute to planning, writing, executing, filming trailer

Elements:

Inclusion of title, author, two short passages from original story

Use of a variety of quality shots

Use of appropriate music

Use of effective voice-over

Effort to convey spirit or theme of story

Effort to be faithful to story plot

No revelation of ending of story: "teaser" only

Final Project:

Introduce trailer to class and show final product

Evaluation:

Based on fulfillment of requirements, above, and quality of final
product

Deadlines:

TBA

GREAT AMERICAN SHORT STORY: MOVIE TRAILER EVALUATION SHEET

(Students viewed all the movie trailers and were given an evaluation
sheet for scoring, part of which determined the final grade.)

Short Story _____
Members of Group _____

Movie Trailer Elements

Rank using the following:

5 - Excellent
4 - Very Good
3 - Good
2 - Could Be Better
1 - Not So Good

Overall Interest of Trailer   _____
Overall Quality of Trailer   _____

Variety of Quality Shots   _____
Appropriate Music   _____
Effective Voice-over   _____
Spirit or Theme of Story Conveyed   _____
"Teaser" Ending   _____

Total Score: _____

Comments:

Appendix C:
Young Adult
Literature Project
(Student Handout)

BURIED ONIONS, WHEN THE EMPEROR
WAS DIVINE, WITNESS

I. SMALL-GROUP WORK—SEE NOVEL WORKSHEET

Discussion of themes, character, setting, plot, language, image of
America portrayed. No group should be larger than four people.

II. PAIR PROJECTS—CHOOSE ONE

A. Two Original Poems

Write two original 30-line poems, rhyming or unrhyming (your choice),
using at least two stanzas, which reflect the spirit and intent of your
novel. The first poem should relate to the first half of the novel, and
the second poem should relate to the second half of the novel. The
poems should show knowledge of the novel, appreciation of it, and
some creativity.

B. ABC Book

Using the letters of the alphabet, make an ABC book/list using each letter of the alphabet and citing appropriate events/ideas/concepts. For example, thinking of *The Great Gatsby*,

> D is for **DAISY**, who was Gatsby's love and inspiration.
> E is for **ENIGMA**, the mystery that was Gatsby.

You can illustrate the alphabet book or use different typefaces to make it visually appealing. Artistic efforts are appreciated!

C. Letter—After the End of the Novel

Have the main character of the novel write a letter five years after the end of the novel to someone significant who may or may not know what happened in the novel. The letter should be two pages, double-spaced and typed, and show understanding not only of the novel itself but of the implications of the events of the novel five years later.

NOVEL WORKSHEET

NOVEL TITLE _____

GROUP MEMBERS _____

Please answer these on separate sheets of paper.

I. Themes
List and describe the themes in your novel. Use specifics; cite page numbers if necessary.

II. Characters
List and describe the main characters in your novel. Use specifics; cite page numbers if necessary.

III. Setting
What is the setting or settings in your novel? To what extent does setting affect the novel? Use specifics; cite page numbers if necessary.

IV. Plot

Outline the plot of your novel, including all major events. You can do this through a traditional outline format, map, timeline, storyboard, or list of events.

V. Language

How would you characterize the language in your novel? Are unusual words or phrases used? Use specifics; cite page numbers if necessary.

VI. Image of America Portrayed

What is the image of America in this novel? How is it different from or similar to other pieces of literature we have studied? Use specifics; cite page numbers if necessary.

Appendix D:
Student Questionnaire

Directions: This is a voluntary, anonymous questionnaire, which is designed to ask you some questions abut the course, Images of America, with Dr. Christenbury. Please take a few minutes to respond—your answers are very important and will be helpful in future courses! Thank you for your time.

SECTION ONE: OPEN-ENDED QUESTIONS

(Please write in the space provided.)

I. Things I particularly **liked** about the course

II. Things I would **change** about the course

III. **Advice** I would give someone taking this course

IV. Comments I would give to Dr. Christenbury—what she seemed to **understand** about teaching this course

V. Advice I would give to Dr. Christenbury—what she **needed to know** about teaching this course

SECTION TWO: COURSE CONTENT

(Please circle the one answer that best describes your feelings.)

(SA—Strongly Agree; A—Agree; NO—No Opinion;
D—Disagree; SD—Strongly Disagree)

$N = 18$

I. PIECES OF LITERATURE WE READ

	SA	A	NO	D	SD
A. Images of America Packet					
I **understood** the literature in this packet.	5	12	0	0	0
I **enjoyed** the literature in this packet.	0	9	1	6	1
I **learned** something from the literature in this packet.	1	10	1	3	2

B. Essay Excerpts: Riis (*How the Other Half Lives*); Rodriguez (*Hunger of Memory*); Barnes (*In the Wilderness*); Blunt (*Breaking Clean*)

	SA	A	NO	D	SD
I **understood** most of these essays.	3	10	1	0	3
I **enjoyed** reading most of these essays.	0	5	2	3	7
I **learned** something from most of these essays.	0	11	1	4	2

C. *Death of a Salesman*	SA	A	NO	D	SD
I **understood** the play.	5	11	1	1	0
I **enjoyed** reading the play.	0	5	6	5	2
I **learned** something from the play.	0	4	4	8	1

D. *The Great Gatsby*	SA	A	NO	D	SD
I **understood** the novel.	5	7	2	1	2
I **enjoyed** reading the novel.	5	5	2	2	3
I **learned** something from the novel.	3	5	3	4	3

E. Short Stories (choice of American classic short stories)

	SA	A	NO	D	SD
I **understood** the short story.	3	10	4	0	1
I **enjoyed** reading the short story.	1	11	3	1	2
I **learned** something from the short story.	1	8	5	2	2

	SA	A	NO	D	SD
F. Novel (choice of *Buried Onions, Witness, When the Emperor Was Divine*)					
I **understood** the novel.	7	10	1	0	0
I **enjoyed** reading the novel.	7	6	4	1	0
I **learned** something from the novel.	4	9	4	1	0

G. Research Paper (topic choice of: date of birth, family history, American literature, American cultural touchstone)

	SA	A	NO	D	SD
I **understood** what I needed to do for the research paper.	6	9	1	0	2
I **enjoyed** the work on the research paper.	3	4	4	2	5
I **learned** something from my research paper.	4	8	2	2	2

II. ACTIVITIES WE DID IN CLASS

A. Journal Writing

	SA	A	NO	D	SD
I **understood** what I needed to do for this activity.	6	8	1	0	2
I **enjoyed** this activity.	3	7	2	3	3
I **learned** from this activity.	1	4	6	6	1

B. Writing of Essays

	SA	A	NO	D	SD
I **understood** what I needed to do for this activity.	4	10	2	1	1
I **enjoyed** this activity.	3	3	3	6	3
I **learned** from this activity.	1	5	4	5	2

C. Vocabulary Study

	SA	A	NO	D	SD
I **understood** what I needed to do for this activity.	4	9	3	1	1
I **enjoyed** this activity.	1	4	4	7	2
I **learned** from this activity.	1	9	3	5	0

	SA	A	NO	D	SD
D. Creation of Movie Trailer (based on short story)					
I **understood** what I needed to do for this activity.	10	5	2	0	1
I **enjoyed** this activity.	6	6	4	0	2
I **learned** from this activity.	3	5	6	2	2
E. Novel Activity (choice of ABC Book/Poetry/Letter)					
I **understood** what I needed to do for this activity.	5	11	1	1	0
I **enjoyed** this activity.	8	6	3	0	1
I **learned** from this activity.	3	7	5	2	1
F. Small-Group Work					
I **understood** what I needed to do for this activity.	3	11	3	0	1
I **enjoyed** this activity.	2	7	5	3	1
I **learned** from this activity.	1	8	6	2	1
G. Large-Group Discussions					
I **understood** what I needed to do for this activity.	4	11	2	0	1
I **enjoyed** this activity.	3	12	2	0	1
I **learned** from this activity.	2	10	4	1	1

Any Other Comments You Would Like to Make:

_____
_____
_____
_____
_____
_____
_____

Works of American Literature Cited

Barnes, K. (1996). *In the wilderness: Coming of age in unknown country*. New York: Random House.

Bierce, A. (1978). Chickamauga. In James H. Pickering (Ed.), *Fiction 100: An anthology of short stories* (2nd ed.). New York: Macmillan. (Original work published 1891)

Blunt, J. (2002). *Breaking clean*. New York: Knopf.

Death of a salesman. (1985). Dir. Volker Schlondorff. New York: CBS Television. 130 min.

Fitzgerald, F. S. (1995). *The great Gatsby*. New York: Scribner. (Original work published 1925)

Hesse, K. (2001). *Witness*. New York: Scholastic.

Lee, H. (1999). *To kill a mockingbird*. New York: HarperCollins. (Original work published 1960)

London, J. (1978). To build a fire. In James H. Pickering (Ed.), *Fiction 100: An anthology of short stories* (2nd ed.). New York: Macmillan. (Original work published 1908)

Malamud, B. (1978). The magic barrel. In James H. Pickering (Ed.), *Fiction 100: An anthology of short stories* (2nd ed.). New York: Macmillan. (Original work published 1954)

Miller, A. (1998). *Death of a salesman*. New York: Penguin Books. (Original work published 1949)

O'Connor, F. (1978). A good man is hard to find. In James H. Pickering (Ed.), *Fiction 100: An anthology of short stories* (2nd ed.). New York: Macmillan. (Original work published 1953)

Otsuka, J. (2002). *When the emperor was divine*. New York: Knopf.

Riis, J. A. (1971). *How the other half lives*. New York: Dover. (Original work published 1890)

Rodriguez, R. (1982). *Hunger of memory: An autobiography*. Boston: David R. Godine.

Soto, G. (1997). *Buried onions*. Orlando, FL: Harcourt Brace.

Steinbeck, J. (1978). Chrysanthemums. In James H. Pickering (Ed.), *Fiction 100: An anthology of short stories* (2nd ed.). New York: Macmillan. (Original work published 1937)

Updike, J. (1978). A & P. In James H. Pickering (Ed.), *Fiction 100: An anthology of short stories* (2nd ed.). New York: Macmillan. (Original work published 1962)

REFERENCES

Aikin, W. M. (1942). *The story of the eight-year study.* New York: Harper & Brothers.

Alexander, J. C. (2004, April). Teacher educators and public schools. *Phi Delta Kappan, 85,* 621–624.

Alliance for Excellent Education. (2005, May 9). Governors seek input from students on redesigning the American high school. *Straight A's: Public education policy and progress. 5,* 7.

Alliance for Excellent Education. (2005, May 23). Survey finds that high school students spend little time on class preparation, almost no time reading. *Straight A's: Public education policy and progress. 5,* 7.

Alliance for Excellent Education. (2005, September 6). Americans on high schools: "In need of improvement!" *Straight A's: Public education policy and progress. 5,* 1–2.

Alliance for Excellent Education. (2005, December 12). Year in rewind: High school reform garners national headlines, but most work done at state and local levels. *Straight A's: Public education policy and progress. 5,* 1–2.

Alliance for Excellent Education. (2006, February 21). High school curriculum best predictor of success in college: Longitudinal study finds reading skills a must for accessing challenging high school material. *Straight A's: Public education policy and progress. 6,* 4–5.

Alliance for Excellent Education. (2006, September 5). Paying double: United States spends over $1.4 billion annually on remedial education for recent high school graduates. *Straight A's: Public education policy and progress. 6,* 1–2.

Alliance for Excellent Education. (2007, February 5). President Bush releases FY 2008 budget: Proposal includes several high school initiatives, but would cut overall education spending. *Straight A's: Public education policy and progress. 7,* 2–3.

America Diploma Project. (2004). *Ready or not: Creating a high school diploma that counts.* Washington, D.C.: Education Trust.

Apple, M. (1985). *Education and power.* Boston: Routledge & Kegan Paul.

Atwell, N. (1985, September). Everyone sits at a big desk: Discovering topics for writing. *English Journal, 74,* 35–39.

Baines, L. A., & Stanley, G. K. (2003, Summer). Disengagement and loathing in high school. *Educational Horizons,* 165–168.

Bassett, L. F. (1998, March). An English class with Emily. *English Journal, 87,* 64–66.

Bergeson, T., & Heuschel, M. A. (2006). *The high schools we need: Improving an American institution.* Olympia, WA: Office of the Superintendent of Public Instruction.

Borko, H., Liston, D., & Whitcomb, J. A. (2007, January/February). Genres of empirical research in teacher education. *Journal of Teacher Education, 58,* 3–11.

Boyer, E. L. (1983). *High school: A report on secondary education in America.* New York: Harper & Row.

Cawelti, G. (1994). *High school restructuring: A national study.* [Abstract]. Arlington, VA: Educational Research Service. (ERIC Document Reproduction Service No. ED366060) Retrieved February 12, 2006, from http://searcheric .org/scripts/texis.exe/scripts/x4/ericdb.bin

Christenbury, L. (2000). *Both art and craft: Teaching ideas that spark learning.* Urbana, IL: NCTE.

Christenbury, L. (2000). *Making the journey: Being and becoming a teacher of English language arts* (2nd ed.). Portsmouth, NH: Heinemann.

Christenbury, L. (2006). *Making the journey: Being and becoming a teacher of English language arts* (3rd ed.). Portsmouth, NH: Heinemann.

Cochran-Smith, M. (2006, March). Ten promising trends (and three big worries). *Educational Leadership, 63,* 20–25.

Commission on the Reorganization of Secondary Education of the NEA. (1918). *Cardinal principles of secondary education.* Washington, D.C.: GPO.

Conant, J. B. (1959). *The American high school today.* New York: McGraw-Hill.

Conant, J. N. (1967). *The comprehensive high school.* New York: McGraw-Hill.

Creeley, R. (1991). A form of women. In *Selected poems* (pp. 47–48). Berkeley: The University of California Press. (Original work published 1962)

Cuban, L. (1993). *How teachers taught: Constancy and change in American classrooms 1880–1990* (2nd ed.). New York: Teachers College Press.

Cuban, L. (2001). Introduction: 1980–2000 The bottom line. In Sharon Mondale & Sharon B. Patton (Eds.), *School: The story of American public education.* Boston: Beacon Press.

Daiker, D. A. (2002). Scriptless in high school: Teaching dreams of a college professor. In Thomas C. Thompson (Ed.), *Teaching writing in high school and college: Conversations and collaboration* (pp. 3–12). Urbana, IL: NCTE.

Daniels, H., Bizar, M., & Zemelman, S. (2001). *Rethinking high school: Best practice in teaching, learning, and leadership*. Portsmouth, NH: Heinemann.

Dante, A. (1968). *The divine comedy*. New York: Holt, Rinehart and Winston. (Original work published circa 1308)

Dewey, J. (1961). *Democracy and education*. New York: Macmillan. (Original work published 1916)

Dickens, C. (1965). *Hard times*. New York: Harper & Row. (Original work published 1854)

Dudley-Marling, C. (1997). *Living with uncertainty: The messy reality of classroom practice*. Portsmouth, NH: Heinemann.

Eliot, T. S. (1952). East coker. *Four quartets in The complete poems and plays 1909–1950*. New York: Harcourt Brace & World. (Original work published 1943)

An experience curriculum in English. (1935). A Report of the Curriculum Committee of the National Council of Teachers of English (W. W. Hatfield, Chairman). New York: D. Appleton-Century Company.

Fairbrother, A. (2003, November 26). A teacher's reality check. *Education Week, 23*, 27.

Forster, E. M. (1997). *Howard's end*. Boston: Bedford Books. (Original work published 1910)

Gold, E. (2003). *Brief intervals of horrible sanity: One season in a progressive school*. New York: Penguin.

Goodlad, J. I. (1984). *A place called school: Prospects for the future*. New York: McGraw-Hill.

Hawley, R. A. (1979, April). Teaching as failing. *Phi Delta Kappan, 60*, 597–600.

Hine, T. (1999). *The rise and fall of the American teenager*. New York: Avon.

Hudson-Ross, S., & McWhorter, P. (1995, February). Going back/looking in: A teacher educator and a high school teacher explore beginning teaching together. *English Journal, 84*, 46–54.

Hynds, S., & Appleman, D. (1997, December). Walking our talk: Between response and responsibility in the literature classroom. *English Education, 29*, 272–294.

Kennedy, M. M. (2005). *Inside teaching: How classroom life undermines reform*. Cambridge, MA: Harvard University Press.

Lewis, A. C. (2004, April). High schools and reform. *Phi Delta Kappan, 85*, 563–564.

Lewis, A. C. (2007, February). Movers and shakers, then and now. *Phi Delta Kappan 88*, 419–420.

Martinez, M., & Bray, J. (2002). *All over the map: State policies to improve the high school*. Washington, D.C.: Institute for Educational Leadership.

McDonald, J. P. (1992). *Teaching: Making sense of an uncertain craft.* New York: Teachers College Press.

McNeil, L. M. (1986). *Contradictions of control.* New York: Routledge & Kegan Paul.

McNeil, L. M. (2000). *Contradictions of school reform: Educational costs of standardized testing.* New York: Routledge & Kegan Paul.

Meier, D. (1995). *The power of their ideas: Lessons for America from a small school in Harlem.* Boston: Beacon Press.

Melville, H. (1970). Bartleby, the scrivener. In Warner Berthoff (Ed.), *Great short works of Herman Melville.* New York: Harper & Row. (Original work published 1853)

Michie, G. (2005). *See you when we get there: Teaching for change in urban schools.* New York: Teachers College Press.

Newkirk, T. (2003). The learner develops: The high school years. In James Flood, Diane Lapp, James R. Squire, Julie M. Jensen (Eds.), *Handbook of research on teaching the English language arts* (2nd ed.). Mahwah, NJ: Lawrence Erlbaum.

Newkirk, T. (1992). Silences in our teaching stories: What do we leave out and why? In Tom Newkirk (Ed.), *Workshop 4: The teacher as researcher* (pp. 21–30). Portsmouth, NH: Heinemann.

Nieto, S. (2003). *What keeps teachers going?* New York: Teachers College Press.

Noddings, N. (1992). *The challenge to care in schools: An alternative approach to education.* New York: Teachers College Press.

Powell, A. G., Farrar, E., & Cohen, D. K. (1985). *The shopping mall high school: Winners and losers in the educational marketplace.* Boston: Houghton Mifflin.

Shulman, L. (2000, January). From Minsk to Pinsk: Why a scholarship of teaching and learning? *Journal of the Scholarship of Teaching and Learning, 1,* 43–53.

Sion, R. T. (2006, August). The irresponsibility syndrome. *English Leadership Quarterly, 29,* 10–12.

Sizer, T. R. (1984). *Horace's compromise: The dilemma of the American high school.* Boston: Houghton Mifflin.

Sizer, T. R. (1992). *Horace's school: Redesigning the American high school.* Boston: Houghton Mifflin.

Sizer, T. R. (1996). *Horace's hope: What works for the American high school.* Boston: Houghton Mifflin.

Thompson, T. C., & Louth, R. (2003, September). Radical sabbaticals: Putting yourself in danger. *College Composition and Communication, 55,* 147–171.

Toch, T., Jerald, C. D., & Dillon, E. (2007, February). Surprise—High school reform is working. *Phi Delta Kappan, 88,* 433–437.

U.S. Department of Education. (1983). *A nation at risk*. Washington, D.C.: USOE.

U.S. House of Representatives. (2005, May 17). High school reform: Examining state and local efforts. Hearing before the Committee on Education and the Workforce. Serial No. 109–16. Washington, DC: U.S. Government Printing Office.

Warner, M. (2004, December 3). Remarks for U.S. Department of Education's 2nd annual national high school leadership summit. Washington, D.C. Retrieved March 28, 2006, from www.ed.gov/about/offices/list/ovae/pi/hs/natsummit.html

Willis, P. (1977). *Learning to labour*. Westmead, U.K.: Saxon House.

Index

ABOUT THE AUTHOR

Leila Christenbury is a veteran high school English teacher and professor of English Education at Virginia Commonwealth University, Richmond. The former director of the Capital Writing Project, she served as editor of *English Journal*, president of the National Council of Teachers of English, and was a member of the Steering Committee of the National Assessment for Educational Progress (NAEP).

The author of *Making the Journey: Being and Becoming a Teacher of English Language Arts*, Christenbury is a frequent keynote speaker across the country and has been quoted in the New York *Times*, the *Washington Post*, *USA Today*, *U.S. News & World Report*, and the *Chicago Tribune*.